A REBIRTH

A REBIRTH

Poems by
Foroogh Farrokhzaad

Translated from the Persian by
David Martin

Critical essay by
Farzaneh Milani

Illustrated by
Azar Hicks

Mazda Publishers
1997

Mazda Publishers
Since 1980
P.O. Box 2603
Costa Mesa, California 92626 U.S.A.
http://www.mazdapub.com

ISBN:0-939214-30-X

TRANSLATOR'S FOREWORD

at four o'clock
Forooq is at the cross
               roads
getting nailed
getting pinned under
               another car*
going beyond being
               just another scar
getting smashed up beyond recall
               to the living
going under
       the murky smirk
       of death's unconsciousness

considering the traffic in Tehran
that is not an unusual mess
nonetheless
       the slush
is turning red
from a dead
       poet's blood

all of us who come later
do not exist for her
but I like to think
I can do the dead a favor

---

*At the time of writing this foreword in Tehran, I was misinformed about the actual circumstances of her death, many rumors being in the air. See Introduction.

TABLE OF CONTENTS

INTRODUCTION

A Rebirth (Tavallodi Digar) is the masterpiece of the late Foroogh Farrokhzaad (1934-1967). Her first name (Foroogh) means, "brilliance, radiance," and her last name (Farrokhzaad) means, "born with cheeks (face) shining with glory." Her voice was already the most significant voice in women's poetry in this century in Iran—some say she was the greatest poetess in the long history of Persian Poetry (from the tenth century A.D.) to modern times)—when her life was cut short by an automobile accident at age 33. Indeed, the only other names of Iranian (Persian) poetesses which come to mind are: Raabe'eh, the first Persian poetess of note, some nine centuries ago; Qurrat al-'Ayn ("Gleam of the Eye") also known as Taahireh, Babi martyr in the middle of the last century who wrote religious (devotional) love poetry; Parveen E'tesaami who flourished towards the end of the last century, writing sentimental poems from within the seclusion of women's life of those times; the guerilla martyr Marziyah Ahmadi Oskoo'i; and Taahireh Safaar Zaadeh, a contemporary apologist for Islam. When Foroogh died—in Iran one often refers to a favorite poet, especially a modern one, by his first name, the intimacy between poet and reader being such as it is—when Foroogh died, she was mourned by friend and foe alike—she had many foes critical of her "immoral" love affairs and others who merely didn't like her poetry because it was new and strange. Yet when her voice fell silent and could be heard no more, it was generally recognized that it was a *great* voice which was no more. The price of such poetic stature was high though, in the coin of unhappiness and much futile searching (for a deep and lasting love among other things).

Foroogh was married in her teens and already divorced in her early twenties. Socially, that was the first count against her. The boy she bore from that marriage, Kaamyaar (meaning, "Desired Friend"), is the only child of hers to survive her. Though she was later pregnant again, the child did not survive (see the poem, "Red Rose," p. 101). She later adopted a boy, Hassan, who also survives her. She wrote during her marriage and continued writing throughout the series of love affairs she had thereafter, not a few of the affairs being with writers who had no little literary influence on her. Her first books were popular and allowed her some financial ease. In her mid-twenties she took up film-making. Although several of her films were completed and marketed (*A Fire, The House is Black, Water and Heat*, among others, the second being a documentary which was awarded a grand prize in a film festival) her major impact was not felt there.

Love and art, especially poetry, were inextricably woven together in the fabric of Foroogh's life. She was looking for a great love, one to which

she could commit herself fully, one which would give weight to her life.
As she grew older, she felt herself to be more and more isolated from tra-
ditional values and pursuits, and thus, more and more cut off from other
people. This in turn meant she got less and less feedback and support from
people in everyday life. In desperation, she sought a lover to stand by her
and with her. None did (for very long). The "infamy" of her affairs was
bruited about and she felt, in consequence, more cut off from society and
hence more desperate. It was a vicious cycle, not mollified by support
from other women, for there was no women's movement in Iran in the
fifties and sixties. She was a leading lady without a supporting cast, with-
out the unity of community. The loneliness and alienation she suffered,
from *A Rebirth* onwards was both brutal and devastating. Nonetheless,
there were triumphs in her struggle for sexual and emotional liberation
from the constraints of her society, as "Conquest of the Garden" (p. 72)
so amply demonstrates. In this poem, she achieves a purity of sexual love
which allows her to let it shine despite the press of ill-wishers about her
who would consider this love to be illicit. She had finally flung off her
latent guilt about extra-marital love and no longer felt as if she had to
hide it. (I am indebted to Farzaneh Milani for her comments on this
poem.)

Characteristically, as with all true artists, her alienation and desperate
search for a deep and lasting love drove her art on to new heights. With
A Rebirth (published in 1342 A.H./1963 A.D. and reprinted almost every
year since then), she had reached a new level of poetic mastery and tried
to repudiate the sense of her three earlier books of poetry: *The Prisoner*
(1334/1955), about the suffocating traditional life of Iranian married
women; *The Wall* (1335/1956), about the resistance she met trying to
be a woman and a person outside of the marital context; and *The Revolt*
(1337/1958), about her metaphysical rejection of the traditional Muslim
concepts of the nature of good and evil. Her poetry up to that time had
been well crafted and some of it simply beautiful, but it lacked breadth
and depth. She found that breadth and depth in *A Rebirth*. She developed
a kind of *personal* love poetry, practically introducing that genre into
Persian Poetry. (Impersonal love poetry, both secular and mystical, has
been highly developed in Iran for centuries.) She was the first Persian poet
to write poems entirely in colloquial. She has been the only poet in Iran
to deal with sexual love explicitly (with the recent exception of the late
Sohrab Sepehry who still tended to approach sex with symbols), but never
without devotion. She has also been the only poet in Iran to write poems
about children, and her own childhood.

The influences on Foroogh's poetry were many and various. The first
and most lasting influence was the poetry of Neema Yoosheej (1895-
1959) who is considered by many to be the father of modern Persian

Poetry. The second major influence was that of Alfonsina Storni (1892-1938), an Argentine poetess who gained fame in 1921 but who eventually, at age forty-six, committed suicide. (Some of her poetry was translated into Persian by S. Shafa, appearing in the book *Shaa'ireh-haa*, "Poetesses".)

Most of the later influences on her poetry came from her peers, contemporary Iranian poets and prose writers, some of whom were undoubtedly her lovers at one time or another. Ibrahim Golestan, to whom *A Rebirth* was dedicated (see "To I. G.," and the title poem, "A Rebirth," p. 197) is perhaps the most subtle and lyrical of contemporary Iranian short story writers. His influence was seconded by that of Sohrab Sepehry, a nature mystic and the leading mystical poet of Iran in this century, author of *The Expanse of Green* (which I have also translated and hope to see in print shortly). "Those Days" (p. 1) and "Question" (p. 32) show his influence. An influence in Foroogh's love poetry was made by a sometime lover of hers, Hooshang Ebtehaaj, better known under his pen name of H. A. Saayeh (see "Ghazal," p. 16). Ahmad Shaamloo, author of *Elegies for the Earth*, *Phoenix in the Rain*, etc., and who may or may not have been one of her lovers, was probably an influence in both the political and depressive tendencies of Foroogh's later poetry. (See "Forgive Her," p. 21, and note no. 1, p. 104.)

A Rebirth, marking the deep grooves of a settled alienation (see "Couple," p. 72; "You Were Killing Me," p. 94; "Amidst the Darkness," p. 20; "In the Green Waters of Summer," p. 17, "Bog," p. 50; and "Green Fantasy," p. 66) and also the satisfaction of somewhat coming to grips with that alienation in an artistic way (see "I Shall Salute the Sun a Second Time," p. 92, and "A Rebirth," p. 97) contains various unique poems, or at least poems singularly masterful in their particular genre. Among the political poems we may point out "O Land Full of Jewels" p. 86), "Earth Signs" (p. 52) and "In the Green Waters of Summer" (p. 17). "Those Days" (p. 1) highlights her capacity to relive her childhood on paper. "'Ali's Mother Said to Him One Day . . .'" not only explores children's fantasies, it is also one of the few modern poems in Persian written in colloquial or "street speech." Her love poems, which are really her "trademark," include "Ghazal" (p. 16), "Union" (p. 25), "Lovingly" (p. 27), "Barriers" (p. 34), "My Love" (p. 41), and "Conquest of the Garden" (p. 72). Her poems illustrating the dark or downhill side of love include "Travel Poem" (p. 13) and "In the Cold Streets of Night" (p. 43).

Foroogh wrote various poems in her last four years (after the publication of *A Rebirth*), of course. As an epilogue, I have included the most famous of these in which, it is said, she displayed a premonition of her own death in her lover's death. (Actually, the references to her "*yaar*" (lover or friend) are so vague as to make identification of that person's relationship io her shaky at best. It is also unclear whether the figure of the *yaar* is single or composite.) In a sense, this poem, "Let's Bring Faith to the Onset of the Cold Season," is her own swan song though she was probably not fully conscious of the premonition and though the song was sung for another. As the Taj Mahal which Shah Jahan built as a mausoleum for his favorite queen, Mumtaz Mahal, also serves as his own mausoleum (he lost the throne before being able to build the projected black-marbled mate of the white-marbled Taj), so may Foroogh's elegy for her lover serve as her own elegy. (Many poets wrote elegies for her, of course. They are to be found in *Jaavidaaneh*, "For Ever.") We shall here quote a few lines of the elegy, "Let's Bring Faith to the Onset of the Cold Season," to illustrate its uncanny premonition of her own fatal accident.

> time passed and the clock struck four . . .
> wind blows cold down the alley
> and I am thinking about the love-mating,
>   trellis-making of flowers—
>   about buds with anemic stalks . . .
>   and a man passing between damp trees
>   a man whose blue cords of veins
>   have crawled up both sides of his throat
>   like dead snakes.

And,

> ah! how upset people get at accidents at intersections
> and at shrills of whistles suddenly broken off
> in moments during which a man must be, must be, must be
> squashed under the wheels of time—
> a man who passed between damp trees . . .

And, finally,

> I told my mother: "it's all over now."
> I said: "you always thought it would happen,
> I mean, an accident.
> we must send an obituary notice to the paper."

Foroogh Farrokhzaad died around two o'clock on the afternoon of February 13, 1967. A victim of her own hurried driving, she lost control of her jeep while turning a corner near the Old Shemiran Road in Tehran and attempting to avoid a bus. She was thrown from the jeep and killed by concussion. Her death has a legendary aura around it, somewhat due to "Let's Bring Faith to the Onset of the Cold Season." I have heard two other (unconfirmed) reports of her death, one that she was killed by running into a tree on a country road while driving drunkenly and the second that she was killed in a taxi in a snowstorm at the intersection of Saasaan and Kisraa (Khusrow or Choesroes) Streets in the western part of Tehran.

Two elements of sadness mark Foroogh's death. The first, as Sadr al-Din Elaahi has said in *Jaavidaaneh* ("For Ever"), the memorial book of criticism and elegies for Foroogh, is that she had by no means exhausted her mine of poetry. She had just, in her last six or seven years, reached her poetic maturity and had finally found her own voice. She left much of her life's work undone. The second element of sadness, as Dr. Reza Beraahani says in the same memorial book, is that no woman's voice has risen in Iran to take Foroogh's place and no young poetess shows promise of being able to be a voice of focused eloquence for Iranian women. This is even more so with the advent of the anti-feminist regime of Khomeini. (It would be well to point out that after centuries of poetry's dominance over prose in Persian Literature, the balance has changed somewhat, but Iranians still look to poetry for the highest expression of truth(s)—that is, besides the religious element which has traditionally reserved the domain of truth to the exclusive compass of the *Koran* and derivative Islamic religious works. The short story, under Hedayat, Chubeen, and Golestan has come close to rivalling poetry, but the novel has not yet come into its own in Iran as a vehicle of literature.) It would be a mistake to label Foroogh Farrokhzaad as just the leading poetess of Iran, for some of her poetry, especially from *A Rebirth* and after, is of the finest poetry modern Iran has given to the world. (This is not the place to discuss the great influence of Persian Poetry in world literature, epsecially in Asia, but by way of comparison, or rather, contrast, with America, Iran is a place where the love poems of Haafez were commonly arranged and sung by *popular* singers almost to this day, over five hundred years after his death.) Yes, Foroogh's voice was the leading voice of Iranian women, but its strength was not just lent to them, but to all Iranis struggling to enter, and to come to grips with, the modern world,—a voice for all peoples who still have one foot in the swamps of the past centuries and one tentative foot in the Industrial Age, —and finally, a voice for all the rest of us who are well-nigh footloose on the "freeways" of our century, men and women both.

to I. G. [1]

all my existence is a dark sign
                    a dark verse [2]
that will take you by itself
again and again
through incantation of itself
over and over
to the dawn of eternal bloomings
                    and eternal growth
in this verse, in this sign, I versified
you, I joined you
to tree and water and fire

THE POEMS

THOSE DAYS

i

those days gone by
those good old days
those days, safe but heady
those skies full of sparkling spangles
those groves full of black cherries
those houses which leaned   *Reliance*
against each other
hiding behind green screens of ivy
those roofs of playful kites
those lanes giddy
with perfume of acacias
those days gone by
in those days my songs
were bubbling up from the slits
between my eyelids
like bubbles filled to bursting with air
my eye took in everything
my eye drank it
        all up like fresh milk
the restless rabbit of happiness
was in each of my pupils
every daybreak with the old sun,
it would go a-searching on strange, unknown plains

An enclosed space
of comforts

nights it would go down
into jungles of darkness
those days gone by
in those silent snowy days
each moment would find me staring out
from behind the window
                        in the warm room
like soft down
my clean pure snow
would come down
gentle and slow
on the old wooden ladder
on the slack rope
                        of the clothesline
on the tresses of elderly pine
and I was thinking of tomorrow
ah, tomorrow
a white slippery mass

                        tomorrow
would start with the rustling
shish, shish of my grandmother's chador[1]
and with the appearance of her distorted shadow
disarranged in the door frame
                        which shadow
would suddenly free itself
in the cold sensation of light —
and the looping outline of flying pigeons
in the stained-glass window panes
tomorrow . . .
the footwarmer's heat was soporific
out of my mother's sight
I would quickly and boldly

erase the lines my teacher made
through my old drills.
when the snow would stop and settle
I would walk around in the garden depressed
I would bury my dead sparrows
down at the bottom of flower
pots of dried-up lilacs

ii
those days gone by
those days of ecstacy and wonder
those days of sleeping and waking states
those days every shadow held a mystery
every closed box held a treasure hoard
in the silence of noon, every closet corner
was a world in
                        itself. whoever
was not afraid of the dark
was a champion in my eyes
those days gone by
those days — those Nouruz holidays[2]   20 March
that expectancy of sun and flowers
those tremors of perfume
in the quiet and coy assembly
of wild narcissus — those innocent wildflowers
who used to visit the city
in the last morning of winter
street peddlars' hawking songs
in the long streets with green
stains

the bazaar was floating in stray smells
in the pungent smells of coffee and fish
the bazaar was being flattened under foot
it was stretching, it was mixing
with all of the moments along the way
and it was spinning, at the bottom

Iranian
new year

4

of dolls' eyes it was Mother
who would go quickly towards
                    flowing colored masses
and come back with gift packages
                    with full baskets
the bazaar was rain which would pour
pour, pour

iii
those days gone by
those days bedazzled in the secrets of the body
those days of cautious acquaintanceship, with
water-colored, blue-veined beauty
a hand which with
one flower from behind a wall, called
another hand
small ink splots on this uneasy,
anxious, fearful hand
and love
which in a shameful "hello" would repeat
and demonstrate itself
in hot smoky noons
we read our love
letters traced in the alley
                    dust
we were familiar with the easy
simple language of messenger flowers[3]
we carried our hearts to the Garden of in
nocent affections. and we loaned
our hearts to the trees
and the ball was passed
around in our hands
with message-kisses
and there was love, that mixed-up feeling
which all at once surrounded us in the darkness
of our alley doorway and attracted
us and melted us in ecstacy
in a thick and bushy crowd of burning

breaths and heartbeats
and furtive smiles

iv
those days gone by
long gone, long gone by
those days like plants which rot in the sun —
from sunshine they wilted and rotted
and those lanes giddy from acacias' perfume
were lost in the shoving
throng of clamorous streets —
streets of no return
                              getting jammed together
and a girl who rouged
her cheeks with geranium leaves . . .
ah! now she is a lonely woman
now she is a lonely woman

TRANSIENCE

how much longer
do I have to go on
                              wandering
from one place to another?
I can't go on, I can't
go on searching
every time another love, another lover
if only we were those two swallows
then we could travel about all our lives
from one spring to another
ah! now it's been a long time
since the dark caved in on me
the dark load of heavy clouds
which dumped, which sunk

their gloom into me
as I mix with your kiss on my lips
I imagine a fading perfume
giving up the ghost

my sad love is so tainted
with fear of ebb, ebb, ebb
that all my life shivers.
when I look at you it's as if:
I am looking from a window
at my only tree, luxuriantly in leaf
in autumn's golden fever
when I look at you it's like this:
I am watching an image
on the surface of swirling currents
                              of floating water
night and day
night and day
night and day

pass! let me
forget

what are you
except
        a moment?   — a moment
which opens my eyes into vivid
awareness of a desert vista

pass! let me
forget

SUN'S SHINING

i

look at
the sorrow in my eye!
look how
drop by drop, the sorrow melts, I cry!
look how black my rebellious
black shadow is captivated by
sunshine's hand!
look! all
       my
being is being ruined, desolated
a spark
       of fire
pulls me to desire
it carries me
to the zenith.
it lays
a trap for me
it pulls me
in, hooked. look! —
my entire
       sky
spills fills up in meteor
ball of flame

ii

Who?

(you) came
from far, far away
from the realm of perfumes and lights   *Heaven?*
you have sat me down now
in the prow of a boat, made
of ivory, of clouds, of crystals   *white & pure*
O my
      tender hope! carry me!
carry me to city of passions
      city of poetry

you pull me
towards the starry
way you seat me
above stars, above the
stars
look! see!
I got burned from the
stars
I was filled to brim
by stars. by stars of fever
like simple-hearted red fish
I came to be
a star-picker of night's pools
long
ago how far
it
was from our earth
to these bruised blue
          blue balconies of sky!

your call
comes to me now for
                    the second time —   *Religious experience*
the call of angels' snowy wings
look where I've reached! — I
have come
to galaxies, to unfathomed vastness,
          to the next
          world

now that we are come on high   *The mixing of*
to the very heights, to the zenith   *pleasure*
wash me with   *and religion*
waves of ocean-wine!
wind me in the fine
silk of your kiss!
desire me
          in the endless
                    drawn-out, stretched-out nights

9

don't release me

                ever again

don't separate me

                from these stars

iii

look how the wax of night on our path,
how it melts drop by drop!
my eyes' black flask
fills to the brim with sleep's wine
fills to the warm sound of your lullaby
look inside
the cradles of my poetry!
you bud! you sprout!
. . . and the sun comes out!

ON THE EARTH (ON THE GROUND)

i

never have I
wanted to become a star
in the mirage of sky
nor have I
wanted to become a si
-lent companion of angels, like
those chosen souls
never have I
been separated from the earth
nor have I
been acquainted with stars
I have stood on the earth
with my body like a plant stalk
—which sucks on sun
and wind and rain-

                water, water to survive

                    sun to stay alive

Earthly
experiences

fruitful from desire
fruitful from pain and strain
I have stood on the earth
for the stars to praise me
for the breezes to caress me

ii
from my peephole I look out
I am nothing more

she does
not wish
to ascend

than the tinkling of a melody
I am not eternal
I search for nothing more
than the tinkling of a melody
in the groan of a delight
which is purer than the simple silence of a sorrow
I am not in search of a nest

Does not
need a
home

a nest in a body which is a dewdrop
a dewdrop on the white lily of my body

iii
passersby drew mementos
on the wall of my hovel,
which hovel is life.
with the black line
             of love,
with the black hand
             -writing of love,
they drew mementos:
          love-
                  pierced heart
             over-turned candle
             faded, the silent faded
                  dots above[1]
             the interlaced and inter-entangled
             letters of madness.

12

every lip which touched mine
                    conceived a star
                    in my night, star
                    which sat on the river of mementos
then why do I pine, then why
do I long for a star?

iv
this is my song
sitting pretty, sitting charm
ingly on my heart's bliss
before this
there was nothing
                    more
                    than this

TRAVEL POEM

i
every night someone would say
                    to my heart:
"You're all torn up from his visit.
Come daybreak, he'll go away
along with white stars.
O, he's going, he's going, hold him!"

I was sent
out of this world by your soul's perfume
unaware of the deceits of tomorrows.
your eyes like gold dust
                    were pouring
                    out onto my delicate eyelashes

13

my body burning
                        —hot from the touch of your hands
my hair liberated in your breath
I was opening from love and said:
"whoever's given his heart to his love
does not mean
                        any harm.
doesn't mean to hurt.
he's going. my eye follows him
he's going. my heart goes out to him.
he's going. let my love hold him!"

ii
ahhh! now you
                        are gone and
sunset spreads
shadows up the breast of the road
gently
        gradually
                the dark
                        turbid god of sorrow
places its foot inside
the temple of my vision
gradually the god
writes on all
                the temple walls
black signs, black verses, all
black, black[1,2]

THE WIND WILL CARRY US

in my small night, what mounting regret!
wind has a rendezvous with the trees' leaves

14

in my small night, there is terror
                              of desolation

listen! do you hear
the wind of darkness howling?
I watch breathless
-ly and wondrously this alien happiness
I am addicted to my own hopelessness
listen! listen well!
can you hear the darkness
howling? —   the dark hell
-wind scything
its way towards us?

in the night now, there is something passing
the moon is red restless and uneasy
and on this roof — which fears
any moment
                    it may cave in —
clouds like crowds of mourners
await to break in rain
                                   ruin
a moment
and then after that, nothing.
behind this window, night shivers
and the earth stands still
behind this window an unknown
something fears for me and you
O you who are green from head to toe!
put your hands
                    like a burning
memory into my loving hands — lover's hands!
entrust your lips — your lips
like a warm sense of being!—
entrust! — your lips to the caresses of *my*
                              loving lips — lover's lips!
the wind will carry us with it
the wind will carry us with it

15

GHAZAL[1]

"every night you listen to my heart's tale
tomorrow you'll forget me like a fabled wail"

—H. A. Saayeh[2]

you listen to my call like stones
    like a deaf wall, dead bones
you are a stone. my words
    didn't strike
they went in one ear and out the other
as if you didn't hear and now
you will forget.
through temptation's blows, you confuse
the peephole's dream sleep
with an early spring shower
you make my hand embrace dead leaves —
my hand which is the caress of the erect
    green stalk.
further from the winey spirit you stray
and you thrust the eye
into the flame. you stupefy the eye.
O you golden fish of my blood's bog![3]
may your drinking spree
    be happy, for that
you are drinking me!
you are the violet valley of sunset
you press the day against your breast
you squash, you extinguish it
your light sat[4]
    in the shadows
    and its color fled,
    was lost to the shadow[5]
    how came it to this pass,
    that you caused her to wear black?

IN THE GREEN WATERS OF SUMMER

i

more lonely
more lonely than a leaf
with my load of joys, aloof
in the green waters of summer
I sail, peace at the helm
I sail:
> to death's realm
> to shore
> > of autumnal griefs
in a shadow, I let myself go —
> in love's unreliable shadow,
> in the fleeing, escaping shadow of happiness
> . . . less, less
> in the shadow,
> > fleeting, fleeting

nights in which whirls a dizzy breeze
in the low, heartsick sky
nights in which bloody moon-mists twist
and wind in and out
of alleyways of blue veins, filling them.
nights in which we are alone
with the trembling of our souls, alone —
the feeling of being, diseased being
comes to boil in the pulse, foams,
froths in the heartbeat

"there is a mystery in the expectant
waiting of the valleys" —
they engraved this on the faces of dread
-full boulders hanging atop mountain peaks
one night they fell, and as they fell
and in their own fell line of descent
> > > they filled
up the mountainous silence
with their own bitter pleading[1]

"the serenity of empty hands
is absent
         from hands
full with commotion, handsful of restl
                                essn
                                     ess.

the desolation of ruins is beautiful" —
this came from a woman singing in the waters,
in the green
           waters of summer,
as if that woman were living in ruins

we contaminate and stain
each other with our breath
we are stained with the pure piety of hap
                                        piness
we shrink in fear from the sound of the wind.
we flinch under the influence of shadows of doubt
in gardens of our kisses we fade, fade away
at all the glittering parties of light's palace
we tremble from dread of its collapse[2]

ii
now you are here, spread
           like the perfume of acacias in morning lanes,
           heavy on my breasts
           hot in my hands
           released from yourself in my hair
                      burned out, stupefied
now you are here

something broad and dark and thick
something confused like the far-off noise of day
turns and spreads itself across my nervous pupils

perhaps I am being taken from the spring
or from the source
perhaps I am being plucked off a branch

19

perhaps I am being closed like a door
to subsequent moments.   perhaps . . .
I don't see anymore

iii
we grew on waste land
we are raining on waste land
we saw "the Nothing" on the highways
travelling in state like a king — "the Nothing"
on its own winged pale horse[3]

what a pity! we are happy and serene
what a pity! we are sad and subdued —
happy, because we love
sad, because love is a curse

AMIDST THE DARKNESS

amidst the darkness
I called you
there was silence
there was silence and the breeze
which parted the curtains in the bored
and tepid heavens. wasted heavens.
a star was burning out
a star was going out
a star was dying out
I called you.
I called you.
my entire being
was a glass of milk between my hands
the moon's blue glance
looked down and
got caught in the glass

a morose song was rising
                    like smoke
from cricket town — was drifting like smoke,
curling up the window panes

all the night there
someone was pant- panting
from hopelessness in my lungs
someone was standing up
someone wanted you
two cold hands
pushed her back down

all the night there, from black branches
a sorrow splashed down
someone was neglecting herself
someone was calling you
air was bearing down on her
air was caving in on her

my small tree
was lover to the wind
to the homeless wind
where is the home of the wind?
where is the home of the wind?

FORGIVE HER[1]

forgive her
her who from time to time
forgets the painful grafting of her existence
onto stagnant waters and the pits. empty pits.
she foolishly supposes
that she has a right to exist

21

forgive her
forgive the indiscriminate fury of an image
in which the remote desire of movement
melts in its papery
eyes

forgive her —
the current of the maroon moon
flows down all the way through her casket
and the upsetting breath-taking perfumes
disturb her body's thousand years' sleep

forgive her
her who from within
is demolished. but still the skin
of her organs of sight
burns from the notion of particles of light
and her futile hair quivers shivers hopeless
-ly under the influence of love's breaths
O you dwellers in the simple realms of happiness!
O you companions of windows opened in the rain!
forgive her
forgive her
because she is ensorcelled
because the roots of your fuitful
being . . . tunnel
down into the soil of her exile
and swells her sucker heart
with noxious beats of regret
in the corner of her breast

PERCEPTION

i

in the tiny lampglobe, light's glow
was tiring itself out and fading
all at once the window filled with night
the night overflowing with a mob of empty,
                              voided noises
the night poisoned
            with contaminated exhalations --
                              death's breaths
the night . . .
I listened
in the dark, terror-struck street
somebody's heart squashed underfoot
like a decayed mass of goo
in the dark dreamy street
a star burst
I listened, I heard
my pulse was swollen from a flood of blood
and my body . . .
my body was swollen with temptation
                    to decompose on the spot

on the helter-skelter, any-which-way lines
                        of the ceiling
I saw my own eye
like a heavy tick:
it was drying out from closed mouth,
jaundiced from abstinence: it was paling and trembling,
it was suffocating,
despite all my agitation, I was still slowly . . .
-- like motionless water, stagnation settling in . . .
I was slowly settling down on the bottom
peacefully, peacefully
I was scumming over in my own well

I listened
to my whole life, I listened.

a detested mouse in its own hole
was singing an ugly worthless anthem
shamelessly.
an incessant and meaningless squeaking
was going around and around
a passing moment
and was flattening out
at the level of forgetful
oblivion

O – too much!
O, I was full of lust!
– lust for death
both my nipples were twingeing
from delirium – overbearing excitement
I remember how
on my first day of puberty
my entire being was unfolding
in innocent amazement
to mix with that invisible, that vague, that unknown

ii
in the small lampglobe
light yawned
in a wavering line

UNION

i
those dim, blear eyes, O!–
those simple-secluded Sufis of mine
have popped out of their sockets, staring –
have done gone out of their head, staring
in ecstatic involvement with the dancing
of his two eyes

Spirituality of
Sufism and
the passion
of this
man

25

I saw that he was undulating all over me
like a wave rolling over me
like the red pyramid of fire's blast
like the reflection of water
like a cloud in rain-spasm
like a sky staggering
                    under the breath of hot seasons
as far as the boudless
as far as the other side of life
he had spread
expanding
          he was there   omnipresent
          he was everywhere

I saw that under the blowing of his hands —
his hands blowing like the wind —
the bodyness of my existence was dissolving
I saw that his heart
was winding around
                    the inside of my heart —
was filling up my heart
with its sorceror's wandering echo
with its sorceror's amazed tinkling   magic

time flew
the curtain went off with the wind
I had squeezed him in the conflagration's halo, squeezed
him, I wanted to speak
when all in a wonder
his bushy, shadow-spreading eyelashes
like tassels on silk curtains —
flowed from the root of darkness
in the extension of that stretching, length-searching thigh —
in that spasm, that death-
                    tainted spasm — flowed
to lost limits of my being

26

I saw that I was breaking
                    free
I saw that I was breaking
                    free

I saw that my skin was splitting
bursting from love's expansion
I saw that my fiery mass
was slowly melting, slowly melting from its volcanic peak
and was drip, drip, dripping
into the moon, the moon
settling down into the deep
                    groove
dim and blear the typhoon moon,
into the moon, my liquid love moved,
                              discharged.

ii
we had cried
            into each other
we had lived out the entire unreliable
moment of union in each other
in reckless madness, that passion

LOVINGLY

i
O you! you've colored night with your dream!
my breast has become
heavy from your overbearing
                    scent
O you! you've spread yourself across my eye!
you've given me more joy than sorrow
like a rain which washes off earth's body

you've purified my being from contaminations
O heartbeats of my burning body!
a fire in the shadow of my eyelashes
O you who are more
                    brimming than wheatfields.
O you who are heavier with fruit than golden branches
O you are a door
                    opened to suns, suns
in the pitch black attacks of hesitations!
when I'm with you there's no more
dread of pain
if there be any, it is nothing but
the pain of my happiness
how do my depression
and my load of light
fit into the same picture?
how life's hubbub in the grave's abyss?

O you whose two
eyes are my grass meadows! —
the branding iron of *your* eye
marked *my* eyes!
if I had had you
in my heart before this, I
wouldn't have imagined everyone else to be *you*
the pain of wanting is a dark
                    pain:
         running around and useless exercises in diminishing
                                             oneself
         laying your head down on the dark
         hearts of chest after chest
         contaminating, tainting
         your breast with pus of malice,
                    slime of spites
         finding snake fangs in fondling
         finding poison dripping from your lovers' smiles
         putting gold in the hand of robbers
         getting lost in the expanse of bazaars

28

O you who are mingled with my soul!
O you who raised me up from my grave!
my loneliness was snuffed out —
my loneliness like the star come
come on two gold-plated wings
from the far-off sky —
by your hand my loneliness was put to death.
my body took on the smell of caress
-ing, of embracing, of love
                              -making, smell that
hot jelly roll roll roll
you are the torrent for my veins' riverbed
                              a flood, roiling.
my steps take the road
with your steps in a world
so black and cold

O you who are hidden
                    under my skin
you've become just like the blood boiling
                                        in my skin
my tresses burned away by your caresses
my cheeks wind-burnt by the sweeps
across them by the hot breath of your yearning
ah! O
you who are so
unfamiliar with my shirt!
you are so familiar with my body's grasslands!
ah! O
          bright
                  dawn, sunsetless!
torrid zone's sun
ah! ah! O more suck
                        u
                          lent than early morning!
fresher, more
          thirst-quenching than springtimes
this is no longer love, this
is dazzling wildness —

29

                         this
is a chandelier in the silence and darkness
when love became awake in my breast,
my body gave way from searching
        to giving
        gave, gave way from head
        to toe   this
this is no longer me, no
                         longer me
such a pity I only subsisted
with my myself — what a waste!
such a pity I put up with it —
I called *that* life ? ! ?
you
for whom my lips are the touch
                    point for your kiss!
my eyes stare down the road of your kiss,
                    dazzled.
                         O
you who are the spasms
        of pleasure in my body!
the lines of your body
                    are my shirt. ah, O
I want to
        burst
            out! ah, O
I want my joy
            to be stained sore
                         with sorrow
                         for just one
                         moment
ah! I
     want to get up
I want to   cry
            like a cloud,
            sob-sobbing in downpour
            sob-sobbing heaves, breathe heave breathe
                         pores pours

                         30

over here you've got this sad heart of mine
and over there you've got smoke
                        smoke of aloes wood . . .
how you going to get them mesh
                        together, O.K.?
there ain't no way.
now dig this: in this monk's dormitory
                is there the sweet sound of music
                do you hear the sweet sound
                of jiving harp and rood?[1] my man on the rood
                doing it right there live and jive and they's JAMMING!
                do you here that kind of music here?
                —in this monk's dormitory? ain't no way!
O.K.? and now here in this empty space
                is there any flying? fat chance, jack!
in this night of dead calm
                is there any song?
                ain't no way there's any song.

ii
O! your lullaby
                glances that rain magic!
you eye me with the eye
of some naughty baby-wabie's cradle.
O! your breaths are sleepy breezes
which cleansed anxious shivers, peeled
                        them right off of me.
O you who've been asleep
in the crook, in the upturned
                        smile of my tomorrows!
O you who've gone down
into the depths of my worlds!

O you who've mixed me
with passion of poetry!
O you who've poured
all this fire on my poetry!
since you rubbed and rubbed and kindled

31

my love's fever, of course
you had to end up by putting my poetry
to the torch!

QUESTION

hello fish . . .   hello fish
hello goldens, greens, reds —
tell me:
in that crystal room, the one
which is as cold as the pupils of the dead's
                                        eyes —
which is like afterhours
                    in late city nights
stores and shops all locked up and empty —
in that crystal cold room, tell me now,
have you heard a lip flute's call? —
        a lip flute's call
        which approaches from Faery, the holdout
        of the fairies of loneliness and dread,
        a lip flute's call
        which approaches the brick trust of sleeping bedrooms
        approaches the lullaby of wind-up clocks
        approaches the glass
                        pit-seeds of light —
have you heard a lip flute's call?
        do you hear it now,
                        coming?
and as it comes, sparkling silvery-gold corona-stars
from sky to earth fall
and small
        playful hearts burst
        out crying
when they feel that mixed-up sound of a cloudy squall,
        that tear-squeezing sound of a lip flute's call

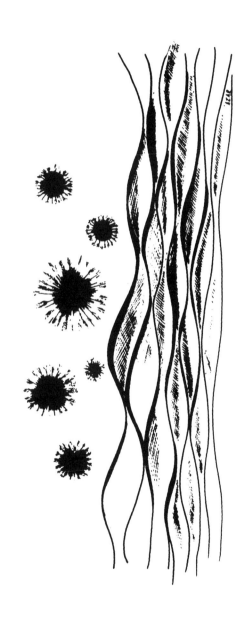

coming on
have you felt it yet? – that lip flute's call?
it's coming closer now

BARRIERS

i

again now in the silent night
retaining walls, boundary walls
grow taller and taller like plants
to stand guard in my field of love
again now

again now the city's foul uproar
migrates from the pitch
darkness of my shore
like a disturbed school of fish
now again windows refind
themselves in sexual contact with
                                 dispersed scents
now again the trees, all
of them asleep in the garden, discard
                           their bark
and the ground pulls in
giddy moonspecks
through thousands of holes

ii

now
come closer
and listen
to the anxious throes and blows of love
which inspissate and fill space
like the tom-tom of Negro congo drums
in the chanting of my organs' tribe

me, I feel
I know
which moment is the moment
of worship
now all the stars
nestle together in sleep

I, in night's refuge, I blow
from the ends
                of all breezes
I, in night's asylum, I collapse,
sink down
                madly with my heavy hair
in your hands. and I present you
with tropical flowers of this
young hot green heat: me.
come with me, come
with me to that star, come! –
to that star so far
eons and eons far
from the solidification of earth
and futile criteria down
                on the ground
no one there
                way up high
                is afraid of light

I draw breath on floating islands –
islands on the face of the waters
I
am in search
of a portion of the expansive wide
sky –
that part I seek
should be free from backlogs of humdrum
and vile ideas

make up with me
return with me
    to the body's beginning
    to the perfumed nucleus of an embryo
    to the moment in which I was created
              from you
make up with me
I remain
        uncompleted by you
now the pigeons fly
from the peaks of my tits
now in the cocoon of my lips
butterflies of a kiss
have sunk
into the thought of emerging
    to fly
      and spread
          their wings
now my body's *mihrab*[1]
is ready for love's worship

make up with me
I just can't say . . .
because I love you
because "I love you" is jive
coming from the world of plastics
and from the crotchety tradition-ridden world
make up with me
I just can't say . . . let me
get pregnant in the night's refuge
let me grow great with child by the moon
let me be filled:
      with small raindrops
      with ungrown hearts
      with globs of unborn children
let me be filled
perhaps my love will be a cradle
for the birth of another Jesus

36

FRIDAY

i

quiet Friday, silent
forlorn Friday, abandoned
Friday like old alleyways, depressing
                pressing down and into the spirit
Friday of sick idle reflections
          catching mentalic light at the wrong angles
          moody broodings
Friday of continual sly yawnings
Friday without expectations
Friday of resignation
             completely down
                    and out

empty house. annoying house.
house closed
to the assault of the young
house of darkness where the sun but daydreams
house of loneliness and omen. house of doubt.
curtained-off house of books, closets, and hallway
                          portraits

ii

my life was like
some strange alien stream
ah! how calmly and self-assuredly
my life passed by . . .
my life was like
          a stream astray
amid the heart of these quiet,
              abandoned Fridays
amid the heart of these empty depressing houses
ah! how calmly and so damn self-assuredly
            my life passed by . . .

WIND-UP DOLL

i

more than this.

                    ah! yes,
it can be even more

                    quiet than this

ii

it can stare down the long
hours with a gaze of the dead,
deadstare-steady
in a cigarette's smoke
it can stare at the design of a cup
and at a faded flower on a rug
it can stare at an imaginary line on a wall
it can pull the curtain to one side
with stiff
and dry
hands and watch:

          a downpour in an alley,
          a kid
          standing with his colored kites
          under an arch;
          sometimes an old rickety push-cart
          hastily and screechingly vacates
          an empty square
it can stand on a spot, dead
still, next to a curtain —
but blind, but deaf

it can cry
in a very lying voice, very alien:
"I love you!"
in the rude strength of a man's arms
it can be a vivacious and attractive female
with a body like a leathern table
                    spread

with two ripe-bulging erect-stiff tits
it can taint the purity of love
in the bed of a drunk,
a lunatic, a vagabond

it can cleverly disdain
any wondrous enigma
it can solve a crossword puzzle all by itself
it can allay its unease by finding a useless answer,
a really useless answer — five or six letters
it can kneel for a lifetime
with head abject at the foot of a cold sepulchre
it can see God in an unknown grave.
with a paltry coin it can find faith
it can rot in a monk's cell
like an old penitent saying prayers of pilgrimage
it can yield an equally worthless result
like zero in addition, subtraction, and multiplication.
in the cocoon of its quarrel
it can take your eye
for the pale and faded button of an old shoe
it can dry up dry dry
up like water in its own well

it can shamefully hide
the beauty of a unique moment
as you would relegate a ludicrous photo —
a black-and-white instant taken in a dilapidated cubicle
— to the bottom of a box
it can hang
the picture of a condemned woman or man
or a defeated, or a crucified, or a hanged
                              woman or man
in a photo frame left empty from some by-gone day
with masks it can overlay
cracks and chinks in walls
it can get mixed up in the most inane plans

not only can it be
like wind-up dolls,
it can see
its own world with two glass eyes
it can sleep
for years in the infolds of spangles and nets
in a felt-lined case
with a body crammed full with straw
it can cry out without any reason at all
with every tug on its string:
"O! I'm so happy!"

THE MOON'S LONELINESS

i

up and down the whole length of darkness:
crickets shrieked,
"Moon, oh great Moon . . ."

up and down the whole length of darkness:
branches which with their outstretched
hands had sent up lustful sighs —
and the breeze submissive to decrees
of divinities allusive and unrecognized —
and thousands of hidden breaths
in the covered-over life under ground —
and in that brilliant itinerant circle,
                            glowworm's nightshine —
anxiety in the wooden ceiling —
Layla[1] in purdah[2] —
frogs in the bogs — :
all of them all together croaked and groaned
monotonously until the dawn,
"Moon, oh great Moon . . ."

up and down the whole length of darkness
the moon blazed in moonlight
the moon was the heart of loneliness
of its own night
the moon was all choked
up in its golden-colored malice
it was about to burst
from sheer pent-up spite[3]

MY LOVE

my love
with that shameless nude
                    body
poised like death
on its powerful forelegs

restless oblique lines
follow the erect design
of his rebellious limbs
my love, he is like
a descendant from lines
of forgotten human races

it's as if
at the corners of his eyes,
there's always a Tartar
lying in wait to spring
an ambush on a mounted rider.
it's as if a barbarian,
in a wet-fresh flash of my lover's teeth
is drawn on by the hot-blood of the hunt

my love has a clear-cut and unavoidable purport,
an indispensable and explicit meaning
like nature.
he confirms the true law
of power with my fall —
he breaks me
                    in.
he is wildly free
like a sound instinct
deep in the interior of an uninhabited island
he wipes off the street
                    -dust from his shoes
with strips torn from Majnoon's tent.[1]

my love
is like a god in a Nepalese temple
as if from the very start of his existence
he has been totally other.
he
is a man of bygone centuries
reminiscent of beauty's true and noble blood

he always wakes
                    up innocent memories
in his own space
like the smell of infancy.
he is like an upbeat popular song
brimming with rough
                    and gutsy bareness

he sincerely loves
          life's atoms
          specks of dust
          human sorrows
          clean griefs

he sincerely loves
          a garden-lane in a village

a tree
a bowl of ice-cream
a clothesline
my love
is a simple man
he is a simple man whom I
have hidden in the sinister realm of wonders —
like the last sign
of an amazing strange religion —
in the inscaped infolds of the bush
under my tits

IN THE COLD STREETS OF NIGHT

i
I'm not scared
I'm thinking about this submission, this
submission tainted with pain.
I kissed
my cross of fate
at the peak of my own mounds,
my own killing grounds.

ii
in the cold streets of night
couples always say good-bye
to each other with hesitation
in the cold streets of night
there's no sound except "good-bye, good-bye"

I'm not scared.
it's as if my heart
were flowing
towards the other side

of time
life will revive my heart
            make my heart
            repeat its heart-beat, heart-beat, heart-beat
and the dandelion which the wind drives
across lakes will repeat me, repeat me, repeat me.
ah! do you see
            how my skin cracks?
            how the milk in the cold blue
                veins of my tits clumps up?
            how the blood begins
                its cartiligeneous growth
                in my patient loins?
you I am
            you. and someone
            who loves and someone
            who inside herself suddenly
            rediscovers a mute link, a grafting
            with thousands of unknown things swarming
            in alieness.
and I am the entire
sharp pang of earth lust on fire
which draws all
                the waters into itself
to make all
                the plains fruitful

catch my far-off cry stark
and fading
            calling in the heavy morning
                                    mists
            calling amidst
                the foggy fumes of morning incantations,
                                    torpid dawn magics[1]
look at me in the silence of mirrors!
look how I explore the dark
                        pit,
all the depths of dreams again,

with the dregs of my hands
and I tatoo my heart
like a bloody stain on the innocent
well-being of being
I'm not scared
O my love, talk about me
with another me whom you'll meet
in the cold streets of night
with the same loving eyes
and the same lover's eyes
and remember me
in her sorrow
                    -ful kiss
on the kind lines under your eyes

IN ETERNAL TWILIGHT

i

is it day or night?
no, my friend! it's eternal twilight,
an eternal sunset with the passing
of two pigeons on the wind
like two white coffins
and far-off sounds from that alien plain
inconstant and wandering like the motion of the wind

ii

something needs to be said
something needs to be said
my heart wants to couple with the pitch darkness
something needs to be said

what a leaden oblivion!
an apple plumets from the branch.

my lover's canaries crush
golden grains of linseed
between their beaks.
in the intoxication of the breeze
the bean plant entrusts
its purple-blue nerves to deliverance
from a mute anxiety of change.
and heɩe, in me, in my head?

ah . . .
there's nothing in my head
'cept the spinning of dots, thick and red
and my sight is like
a false statement, shameful
and fallen — a lowered gaze

I brood over a moon
I mull over a message in poetry,
    think about a fountain
    ponder an apprehension in the ground
    wonder about a rich smell of a wheatfield
    about bread's fable
    about the innocence of games
    and on that long narrow lane
    through which wafted the scent of acacias
I reflect on the bitter waking
which follows on the heels of playing and games
I think in amazement about hypocrisy
flourishing back behind the lane
and I wonder about
the long emptiness stretching in the wake,
lingering after the passage of acacia's perfume

iii
heroics? ah!
the horses are old
love?

love is alone
and looks out on sober, unromantic deserts
from a small window looks out
on a mountain pass with the confused memory
of a delicate cupbearer swaying gracefully
and wearing an ankle-ring
swinging and singing "chink-chink" as she walks

desires?
they're blowing it! they're losing themselves
against a merciless, united front
of thousands of doors . . .
closed?
yes indeed closed! — continually closed. . .
you'll get tired
I think about a house
with its breath of ivy,
limp, lax, and released, a house
with lights bright and flickering,
lights squinting like eyes — a house
with its pensive lazy nights, unruffled
and I think about a new-born baby
with an endlessly widening smile
like concentric circles on water and a blood
-filled healthy body like a grape
                              cluster

I brood over pressures and cave-ins
and black howling pillage, the buzzing shock.
in my mind I question a dubious light
that ransacks the window at night.
I brood
over a small grave,
small like the body of a baby
                    (new-born but new-dead too)

work . . . work?
yes, indeed! but at that great table a hidden
enemy lurks

who chews you slowly slowly as it would chew
wood and notebooks and thousands of other useless things
and finally you go down in a cup of tea, sink
like a boat in a maelstrom
                              and you won't see anything
at the farthest
horizons
except copious cigarette smoke and cryptic lines

a star?
yes, indeed! hundred and hundreds, but
all of them behind bars. night's bars.
a bird?
yes, indeed! hundreds and hundreds, but
all of them in distant
memories:
                proudly their wings'
                futile flapping.
I flash on a scream in the alley.
I reflect on a harmless mouse
which goes into the wall from time to time.

iv
something needs to be said
something needs to be said
in the morning, in the shivering moment
wherein space mixes
                        suddenly with something vague
like the flooding feelings of puberty
my heart wants to give
                        in to the flood
my heart wants to burst
                            into rain
into rain from that great cloud
my heart wants to say:
no! no! no! no!

let's go
something needs to be said
goblet or bed or solitude or dream?
let's go . . .

BOG[1]

i

the night turned
dark. it took sick.
wakefulness flashed incessantly on my eyes
my eye[2] cannot stop seeing, wouldn't you know it!?!
my eye doesn't know how to hide, worse luck!
my eye went and found in me
an ancient death zone,
found my being to be
an ancient expectation. my eye
saw that desert and my loneliness
my eye saw my sun and my moon,
both cardboard and flimsy.
like an old embryo quarreling with the womb
my eye tears the womb walls with its claws.
alive, but longing for birth
dead, but wanting to give up the ghost
conceited from pain
of not wanting
                    itself.
asleep from a passion for standing up
my laugh a futile sadness
my shame comes from my useless pure-heartedness
my heavy exile devolves from giving
my heart away
death's gaudy passion in my love-making
my eye never came down off its high
horse in the

heights my eye
witnessing its own execution
earthmaggot and its dust, but
                              stinking. my eye's
kites in clear skies.[3]
its concealed half goes unrecognized,
ashamed of its human cheek, its humanity.
my eye runs from place to place
in search of its mate
addicted to the scent of its mate
it finds him from time[4]
to time but not believing in him
its mate however is far
more lonely than she
both of them confused and fearful
of each other; each disappointed
in the other and both ungrateful
their love, a doomed fantasy
their union, a dubious vision

ii
ah! . . . if
there were a way for you and me
to get down to our sea
what leisure, what release
our going down would be!
there would be no fear in going
                              down
                              under . . . but if
water were blocked by a bog from flowing
the water would degrade itself by stagnating
its spirit would become desolated,
                    a ruinous region
its depths would become the grave of fish

gazelles, O gazelles of the plains!
if sometime you find yourselves on a sylvan pathway
say, in an enchanted climax forest . . . O.K.?

now if you were to come across a babbling brook
happily singing away, a brook
flowing towards the independence of oceans,[5]
flowing with the silk of its own swirling, a stream
asleep on its own surging
                    chariot, a stream
with the mane of the wind-horse in its claw
a stream with the moon's maroon soul trailing behind
a stream opening the stalks' thighs so green
a stream stealing the scent of the bushes' first fruits
on this brook's surface, on the eye sheen
of every buble there, in light signed,
reflects back the relentless, but bounteous sunshine
gazelles! O gazelles! ah . . . if
you find this stream
remember that
                    sleepless eye's dream!
remember death in the bog!

EARTH SIGNS

i
that time
the sun turned cold
and grace left the face of the earth

and grasses on the plains withered
and fish in the seas dried up
from that time forth, earth
did not receive its dead
night in all the pale
                    windows
like a blurred image
was bound in the throng and surging press —
bubbling up and
                    subsiding, bubling up and

and roads freed their own
continuations in the darkness

no one thought about love anymore
no one thought about triumph any more
and nobody but nobody thought
about anything anymore
in the caves of solitude
futility came into the world[1]
blood gave off a bhang-and-opium smell
pregnant women
bore headless children
and cradles took refuge from shame
in graves

what black and
                bitter days!
bread had overcome the wondrous
power of prophecy[2]
prophets fled hungry and penny
                                    -less
from divine rendezvous. and stray
lambs no longer heard
the shepherd
calling "hey! hey!
come together!"
in the bewilderment of plains

in the mirrors' eyes
motions and colors and images as it were
were being reflected upside-down
                        and above and
behind heads of sordid buffoons.
                        and around
the impudent cheeks of whores
a brilliant holy halo was burning like a flame
-ing umbrella

54

bogs of alcohol with those
astringent poisonous gasses sucked
down a whole immobile
crowd of liberal thinkers into its depths
and insidious, noxious mice chewed
up gilt leaves of books in old cupboards[3]

the sun had died
the sun had died, and tomorrow —
the concept of "tomorrow" — was vague
and lost
somewhere in children's mute minds.
in their homework they would scribble and exhibit
the unfamiliarity of this old word "tomorrow"
with a large black splotch

the people, the fallen
mass of humankind, dead-hearted and hunched over
dumbfounded and stupefied under the ill
-omened load of their corpses —
they would wander from one exile to another
and the painful desire for crime
was swelling in their hands
sometimes a spark, an insignificant spark
would suddenly destroy this life
                                        -less, deathly still
crowd from within. They were all shoving,
mobbing each other, men were slitting each other
's throats with knives
and they were raping little girls on a red
bed of blood.

they were overwhelmed by their terror of themselves
and the fearful feeling of vice
had paralyzed
their blind and dull
                    spirits

always
in the proceedings of an execution
always when the gallows'
rope was squeezing, squeezing out
the convulsed
eyes of the condemned — was popping out
eyes from eyesockets, they would brood
always would brood and retreat
into themselves
and their old and tired nerves drew
strength from a lustful fantasy
but you would always see
                          these
small-time murderers who stood
around the edges of public squares.
they would   idly stare
at the persevering gushing
of water fountains

ii
perhaps yet again
behind squashed eyes, in the murk, in the
freezing depths of congelation
some mixed
           -up half-living
                  thing had held its ground
and without really taking a close look around
wanted to bring faith to the purity
               of the waters' song.
               perhaps
but what
endless emptiness!
the sun had died and nobody knew that
the name of that
           sad dove
that had fled from hearts — nobody knew that
its name is faith

iii

ah emprisoned cry!
won't the majesty of your despair
ever
dig a shaft towards light
from any direction of this abhorrent night?
ah! emprisoned cry!
O last cry of c r i e s . . .

GIFT

I speak from the extremity of night.
from the far end of the darkness
and from the extremity of the night
I, I speak forth

if you come to my house O kind one
bring for me a lamp
                    and
bring for me a small round window
so I can look out
upon the throng-happy lane

NIGHT VISITATION

i

and the wondrous face said to me
from the far
            side of the window:
"whoever sees is right.

58

I, like a creeping sense of lostness,
         spread dread and heart-catch terror
         wide-eyed panic turned loose, gone wild —
but my God! how come you're afraid
                           of me?
—me who
         has never been anything
but a light   and free
                              -flying kite
above hazy   roofs of the sky
and a mouse with the name
                  of death
has chewed up my love, has chewed
my desire, my hate   , my pain
in the nightly exile of the grave
                  yard"

from moment to moment
the wind wiped out and altered
the flowing forms of the wondrous face
with its soft and fine long-tailed lines.
and her tresses, long and soft
were being carried off
by the secret disturbance of the night
which spread those tresses those long and soft
throughout the up and down the whole
length and breadth of the night
                  just like
plants of the ocean deep
her wondrous face, her tresses long and soft
were flowing towards the small window and cried
out loud: "believe me!
I'm not alive."
beyond her I could see the massing darkness
and I could still see silvery
fruit of the cedar tree
oh! but she . . .

she was slipping on all these
and her infinite heart took off
racing along zenith's reach
like green feel of trees
and her field of vision, her eyesight
kept on stretching, stretching
streaking to eternity

ii

"you're right.
    I've never dared to look
into the mirror after my death
and I'm so far gone
      in death
that nothing proves my death
anymore.
    ah!
did you hear a cricket's chirping
from the far side of the garden —
a cricket that fled towards
the moon in night's refuge?

"I think all the stars
have migrated to a lost sky.
and the city, how quiet
it was. I
    went all up
and down the line, the whole reach
of the city. I didn't meet
      anyone anywhere
except for a group of pale
statues and some street
cleaners who reeked
      of garbage and pipe tobacco
except them
and hang-dog-tired and sleepy
      watchmen

I came face to face with nothing
                                  else.

"awww . . . weary me . . .
I've died and night
even now is like
the continuation of that same
futile night."

the wondrous face stopped
talking. and the feeling of bursting
into tears
made the vast expanse of her two eyes
turbid and bitter

"O you who
            have hidden your face
in the shadow of life's black mask,
life's sad black face
                    veil! —
sometimes your thinking drifts
towards this
                despairing truth, doesn't it?
—that people's lives today are nothing
but slag and refuse husks of live ones left behind
you might
            say that a kid
                            has become old, aged
in its first smile.
the heart — this jimmied inscription
with the original strokes tampered with,
crossed out and written over — this heart
won't trust its own stony credit rating anymore

"perhaps addiction
to existence
and perpetual popping of downers extend
clean and simple human desires, shove them relent
                                            -less
                                            -ly

to the abyss
            of decadence —
            the final
the final
fading away
the final slip
                    o

                  v

                e

              r

                    the edge of the precipice;
                        the endless
                                        d
perhaps they have banished spirit   r
to the seclusion of an uninhabit   ed   o
island.   p
perhaps I have dreamed sound of crick-ets
                            crick-ets
                            crick-ets
so then are these halt-halting trudgers
who've been leaning so long sufferingly on wooden walking sticks
so then are these those
fleet-footed horse-riders?
and are these O.D.'s, wasted
hunch-backed gaunts — are these those
                        holy ones who know,
who know, who stand tall because
their thoughts are high?
then it's true, true, that human   kind
is no longer waiting for a Coming . . . ?
and have young girls in love poked
their eyes out with long embroidery needles? —
their eyes gullible and naive believe
everything they see.

now you can hear the timbre
of the crows' caw (!)   shriek
deep in some pre-dawn sleep
mirrors wake to brain

                              -tingling
                         intelligence
and isolated and lonely
                    forms
surrender themselves to the first yawn
and undergo the hidden assault of sinister
chaos upon chaos sinister upon chaos upon
as they wake up

"awwww . . . such a bummer . . .
I'm standing at the far end
                    of my own chances
with all my memories of pride and blood, blood
which I don't celebrate
except in chanting bloody epics —
and pride which never sank
                              so low
and I listen: not a sound!
and I stare: not a leaf moves!
and my name which was so clean:
"Forooq": light, brilliance —
"never again will the light's ray of my name
    jostle together the dust of graves"

that face shivered. it split
in half. and its hands
                    came
                    beseeching they came out towards
                    me from cracks like
                    drawn-out sighs
"it's cold
and winds make mincemeat of my outlines
is there anybody in this abode
who has come to know his own
desolated wiped-out face and
thereby still has not become terror-struck?

"has that time not yet come?
has that time not yet come

                         65

for the window to be opened opened opened?
. . . for the sky to rain down pouring rain
and for man
at the funeral of his inner man
to weep and pray? "

perhaps it was the bird who screeched
or it was the wind in the trees that shrieked
or it was me, who in facing the dead
                              -end of my own heart,
                    ascended like a wave
                         of regret and pain and shame.
and I could see through those windows
that those two hands, those two bitter reproaches
still stretched out like long drawn-out sighs
towards my two hands, shrank shrank away
into the false dawn's growing light.
and a voice on the cold horizon
cried out: "good-bye!"[1]

GREEN FANTASY

i

all day I cried in the mirror
spring entrusted my window
to trees' green fantasy
my body wasn't containing
the cocoon of my loneliness.
the odor of my paper crown
had contaminated the space of that sunless
                                        realm

ii

I couldn't, I couldn't any more
bird calls, street noises, the sound

of balls getting lost and the fleeting
hue and cry of kids
and balloons dancing — they were floating
up like soap bubbles, they were bobbing
at the end of a stalk of thread
and wind, wind which was panting
as if it was in the pitmost depth of dark
and turbid moments of lovemaking.
they were pressing, pressing
the outworks of my quiet
fortress of trust
and they were calling my heart
from the old cracks

all day my sight was fixed
on my life's eyes
on those two disturbed and fear-haunted eyes
they fled my steady gaze. like liars
they took refuge in the safe
seclusion of my eyelids

iii
what summit, what culmination?
—all of these winding roads in that cold
sucking mouth
never reach the confluence

                          and end,
                          do they?
what did you give me, O
you pure and simple lying words?
and what did you give me, O
you mortification of organs, O
you denial of desires?
if I had put a flower in my hair
would it have been more deceitful than this
fraud, this paper crown which reeks of words
and sits atop my head? No, no, not so.

how the spirit of the desert snatched up my heart!
and how the moon's sorcery drew
me away from the herd's faith!
how my heart grew more incomplete
and no other half completed this half!
how I stood and saw the ground
melt away underfoot melt away
and the warmth of my lover's body dissipate,
waiting in vain for my body!

what summit? what zenith?
give me shelter, O
you uneasy lamps!
give me shelter, O
you well-lit, skeptic houses—
houses in which clean clothes got tangled up somehow
in the embrace of fragrant smoke-paths
on your sunny roofs!

give me shelter, O
you perfect simple women
whose slim

       fin

        ger tips
follow the line at the surface of your skin

                   the line
of an embryo's exhilarating motion under your skin!
air always mixes with the smell of fresh milk
in the cleavage at your open collars.
what peak? what zenith?
give me shelter, O
you fire-filled hearths,
O you lucky horseshoes!
and O give me shelter,
anthems of pots in grime-black
deceit of kitchens! —

O annoying song of the sewing machine –
O day and night spat
between the carpets and the brooms—
O give me shelter all
you greedy loves whose
possessive bed is decorated
with magic water and drops of fresh blood, is decorated by
aching desire for eternal survival

v
the entire day, entire day
slipped away like a corpse on the water
I was progressing
        towards the most terrifying
                                    break-water
                                                rocks
                            sea-cliff
        towards the deepest sea caves
        towards the most carnivorous fish
my back froze stiff like rigor mortis
from a premonition of death
chills ran up and down my spine

I couldn't
I just could not any more
was heard the sound of my footsteps
rising from objection to the road
and my despair had grown
more enormous than my soul's patience
and that spring, and that green
                            fantasy
which had passage through the window, said
to my heart: "look!
you ain't never made no progress
you just been sinking!"

COUPLE

i

night falls
and after nightfall, darkness
and after dark
eyes
hands
and pant pant pant
and the sound of water
dripping drop drop drop
from the faucet

ii

afterwards two red dots
from two lighted cigarettes
glowing in the dark
tick-tock of the clock
and two hearts
and two solitudes

CONQUEST OF THE GARDEN

i

that crow which flew
up above our heads
and dove into the uneasy fantasy
of a vagrant cloud . . .
and its caw-call shriek streaked across
the breadth of the horizon
like a short streamlined spear—
that crow which flew will carry news
of us to the city

ii

they all know
they all know
that you and me, we
saw the garden
from that cold and stern
peephole — they all know
that we picked the apple
from that playful branch
almost out of hands'
                          reach

they're all afraid, they're *all*
afraid, but you and me, we
merged with lamp and water,
water and mirror — and we
                          weren't afraid[1]

hey, I ain't talking 'bout some loose connection
                          between two names
or about making love in old pages
in a notary public's marriage register! —
hey, that's just hogwash!
I'm talking about my happy hair
about burning red anemones
                          of your kisses
and I'm talking 'bout
the intimacy of our bodies
in rolling fits of love's mad, grabbing passion
and I'm talking 'bout the radiancy of our nudity
like fish-scales in water
what I'm really driving at is the silvery life of a song
which the little fountain sings
at daybreak

one night
we asked wild hares

73

in that jungle of flowing green
and we asked pearl-filled oysters
in that cold-blooded roiling sea
and we asked young eagles
on that singularly alien and victorious mountaintop
we asked: what do we have to do?

they all know
they all know we found the way
to the cold
silent sleep of simurghs[2]
they all know
we found truth in the garden bower
in shy glances of some unknown flower
we found eternity in an infinite moment
in which two suns stared-flared, gazed-blazed
at each other and were dazzled dazed

whispering cringefully in the dark
ain't where it's at
open windows and daylight
is where it's at
        and fresh air, a fireplace
        in which trash, you know, useless things
                                    are burned.
here we go now:
        fertile fields yielding a good crop;
        birth and maturity and fierce pride
our loving hands is what it's all about—
our loving hands which have built
a bridge upside the night
arching way over the night,
a bridge made of perfume's wafting
message and breeze and light.
come to the grass meadow
to the wide meadow and call me!
from behind breaths of mimosas
call me the way
a gazelle calls its mate!

curtains are brimming with hidden spites
and innocent pigeons
look down to the ground
from their white-towered heights.

RED ROSE

red rose
red rose
red rose

he carried me to the garden of the red rose
and amidst the darkness stuck a red rose
into my dishevelled hair
and finally he laid me
down with him to sleep
on the red rose's leaf

O palsied paralytic pigeons!
O blind windows! O trees naive,
inexperienced in menopausal despair! —
under my heart and deep
down in my loins, now
a red rose is growing
red rose
red
like a flag in the
Resurrection[1]

Oh yes! I
am pregnant, pregnant, pregnant!

i

Little 'Ali Boy
'Ali little alibi-liar
'Ali started up out of sleep
in the middle of the night
he rubbed his eyes with his hands
he yawned, stretched three four times
he got up and sat
what had he seen?
what *had* he seen?
he had seen a fish in a dream
a fish looking like a heap of two-rial pieces[2]
looking like a strip of fine silk
with a fringe of bead-work
dig! it was like this: the fish was embroidered with silk
on a "Marvel of Peru's" petal
two smooth round diamond ring-stones
were playing "hide and go seek"
in his eyes.
ever so gently
ever so slowly
it was drawing itself along
the water's surface
its fins were caressing the water's face
like exotic Chinese fans

his body's odor, the reek of spanking-new
paper notebooks. smell of a big fat "zero"
with a "two" marked next to it[3]
aroma of holiday nights and the kitchen
and the food cooking for somebody's vow[4]
counting the stars, you in your bed on the roof
fragrance rising up from the rain hitting
the brick patio in the courtyard
aroma of fresh dried fruitcake and chocolate

dig! like there was a glow-pearl[5] moving underwater
like there was the Fairy king's little girl
in a crystal palanquin. she was going on an outing
just a little excursion to lush and verdant upland meadows
they were showering her with flowers
like there was light all 'round her head
perhaps this fish was of the tribe
        of Jann and Fairies
perhaps this fish was a little loose
        like backdoor fish always messing around
perhaps this fish was a fast-passing fancy
whatever it was
whoever it was
Little 'Ali Boy
was lost in his fantasy
            of it
was utterly taken up
            by it

as soon as he stuck out his hand to touch that
flowing color
young light
silver-showing
lightning struck, rain poured and the water
turned black
the ground's belly opened up down under
            the fish's body
the bouquet
of flowers moved away
and turned into smoke. the bright
ingots and gold-plated rays of light
burned and melted away.
again in little 'Ali Boy's head
just like every other night
the sky's napkin full of pears
no fountain   no fish   no dream[6]

ii

the wind was panting in the wind catchers[7]
it was pulling on
the weeping willow's dishevelled hair
and it blew up under Lady Rose's
cotton-print prayer shawl,
which she wore as a houserobe,
so you could see her long legs

on the clothesline:
undershirts and sweatsuits
they explored each other's bodies
with their hands and grew
                more and more excited
as if they kept on being
                filled and emptied by "bad"
                                        thoughts

crickets had
tuned up their musical instruments (and were playing them)
as soon as the wind calmed down
frogs in the depths of the garden broke out
                                in song
the night was like every night
        was like some earlier nights
        was like some other nights
but 'Ali
was under another world's spell
Little 'Ali Boy
had been ensorcelled
he wanted its pure silver
he wanted the fish he'd seen in his dream
he wanted it in his eye
Little 'Ali Boy was left high and dry
with the dream evaporated gone
there was only the water channel left
the gurgling of water into the pool

78

iii

"Little 'Ali Boy
Little 'Ali Boy
may you be spared tossing and turning in bed!
don't forget what Granny Moonlady said
and don't get sucked in! don't fall for some trick!
if you see a fish in your dream, it's O.K. —
don't get all hung up on it! —
what does a dream have to do with a pool of water, hey?
don't do anything which'll make them write your name
            in the books.[8]
don't do anything
            to blacken your talisman, your fate —
            to make the devils put you on their blacklist
water isn't like a dream, a dream
into which a man dives on one side
of the dream and comes out the other
                              endside
water isn't like a dream:
dig! when there's danger at an intersection
the policeman blows his whistle
thank God! your feet are securely on the ground
you aren't blind — nor bald nor feeble[9]
you're safe and sound, 'Ali,
you've got all the advantages
you *can* go to Shah Abd-al Azeem,[10]
get on the steam engine,[11]
take a step, get tatooed, become
one of the roughnecks of Paamenaar[12]
such a pity that man doesn't see all
these beautiful things!
don't get on the see-saw!
don't look into the viewscope!
now the ice cream season has come
cucumber season too, and apple and plum
a couple of days more, in the Takieh[13]

they'll be smiting their breasts
oh, 'Ali! oh, crazy 'Ali!
which is better, a springy bed
or a winding sheet in a mortuary?
(after the corpse has had its salt bath on a slab).
suppose that you too jumped
                          into salt water
you went and caught that wild untamable
gypsy woman in a net
what's a fish worth? – a fish
doesn't turn into faith or bread.[14]
one span of the skin of a fish's body
isn't even enough to make panties for Fatimah[15,16]
as soon as you touch the fish
you stink from head to toe
your stench wafts its way into all the local noses
the world hides its face from you
go to sleep, go to sleep
so you do not do
           futile things –
so you won't try to solve problems
with thoughts worth a wooden nickel
just lay your head down on a pillow,
                 close your eyes
just get your feet into the stirrups, grab
the horn and sit steady in the saddle
we don't really expect you to
actually ride the horse."

iv
the water was losing its patience
it was running out into the footbath.
like he wanted to cry out in the dark:
"O, come *on*!
who are you trying to kid
with that bullshit? – the kind of bullshit
which people dish out

80

who if for once in their lives
they have a dream, it's a dream about
onions and pickles, yoghurt-water and chelo kebab[17]
what does a simple fish have to do
with a cunt-as-large-as-a-trough? —
even a dog would scorn it.
a fish in water beats the water, darts
and twists and turns and
          handpicks the best stars
then whenever it falls into anyone's dream
it weighs down their dreams with those stars
it carries them away, it carries
them away from this depressing world of four walls, —
the sinister insistence of clocks, exhaustion, boredom, —
the noodle-soup world, easy
          fast-talking words and slovenliness —
the world of colic and overeating
          pains and castration pains —
the finger-snapping, the pawing feeling-up world
          with their wedding games and false-modesty
          to uphold —
the world of non-stop go-go
          aimless wandering on the boulevards —
the world in which people enjoy
the Arabic chanting of the *Koran* by chador-turbaned mullas —[19]
the world where you go early in the morning
to the artillery park and parade ground
to watch the hangings —[20]
the world of midnights
when the folk are all broken up
over the story of Agha Bala Khan —[21]
the world in which whenever its god turns
into its alleys, a group of hags stands behind his back,
a bunch of thugs cuts him off in front —
such brave bullies when armed! —
a world wherein everywhere you turn
you hear its radio blaring —
it takes him away, it takes
him away from the insides of this sack,

this sack full of worms, dirt and disease
it takes him away to the clear
and clean blue waters of the sky
it takes him away
to the purity
of the Milky Way."

v

water fell
over the butterfly's head and was now drowning it
Little 'Ali Boy was sitting by the poolside
he listened to water words
it was as if someone was calling 'Ali
from those deeps, from behind the flower-bed of lights
that someone was sighing, slapping
his foot with his cold, sweaty hand to get
'Ali's attention.
it was as if he was saying,
"one, two, three . . .
you still haven't jumped in ? ha! ha! ha!
I swear to God
I am in those turbid watery depths
mark my words, 'Ali!
'Ali, believe me when I say
I swear to God I'm a dreamfish, hey!
I'm having them sweep and mop up the whole corridor
I'm having them flip over the pearl curtains
so that the clean side shows
in suchwise I instructed loyal servants
I also brought my bejewelled palanquin
when we get as far as three or four
post-stations away from here, we'll reach
the ever green grasslands of the sea
we'll come to shepherdless flocks
                    of foam-flecks, whitecaps and salt-spray
to halls of light without end
and to endless palaces shell-wrought with mother-of-pearl
remember to collect seven or eight

pearls on the way
so that when we're idle we can play
                                    jacks
Oh, 'Ali! I'm a child of the sea
my soul is pure, my breath is clean, 'Ali
the sea is right over there
there where the land ends, 'Ali
what has someone who has never
seen the sea
                understood about his life?
I'm tired. my head is blown
from this smell of slime
don't just stand there
playing footsie with yourself!
don't hesitate so much
that we both sink up to our necks into slime!
come on in! jump! dive! —
or else—
I'll have to tell you, Little 'Ali Boy:
'we can't be friends any more.' "

vi
suddenly splash! water welled up and sucked down
all in one big burble —
dig! like the water found its mate and pulled it in
silvery circles
went around and around and got tired
waves rolled back and once again were chained
        to the bottom of the pool
glub glub glub bubble bubble
gurgle spurgle glub bubble glub
some bubbles
went around in a whorl on the water's surface

vii
—"Little 'Ali Boy?"
—"in the garden"

84

—"what are you picking? "
—"prunes"
   prunes from the Eternal Garden Above
will you have a bite?   help yourself—
in the Name of God, eat![22]

THE BIRD WAS ONLY A BIRD

the bird said, "what fragrance, what sunshine, ah!
spring has come and I shall go
in search of my very own mate."

the bird flew from the edge of the patio
like a message
                    flew
                              and was gone
the bird was small
it didn't think at all
the bird was not thrall
to thought
the bird didn't read newspapers
the bird had no debts
                              outstanding
the bird didn't know
any humans

bird in the air, bird
on the wing and above
the lights of danger, bird
was flying at an altitude of carefree ignorance
and it experienced blue
moments madly

the bird, O! it was only a bird

O LAND FULL OF JEWELS[1]

i

I won!
I've registered myself
I got my name to grace the face of an I.D. card
and my existence is specified by a number
so long live number 678
issued from the Fifth Ward, resident of Tehran!
no more fears from any direction
from now on I hold these dear:
      the gentle and protective bosom
          of the motherland, my homeland
      pacifier-nipples of glorious historical records
      lullaby of culture and civilization
      and the clatter-clatter of the law's baby rattle:
      click-clack-cluck!
ah!
no more fears from any direction

from an excess of joy
I went to the window and sucked
air into my lungs six hundred and seventy-eight times
air thick with dust and stink of rubbish
and urine, longingly I breathed this constipated constricted
air six hundred and seventy-eight times
and under six hundred and seventy-eight I.O.U.s
and on six hundred and seventy-eight work applications
               I signed
               Foroogh Farrokhzaad

hey! ain't it great! I mean
it's a grace to subsist
in the land of poetry and flowers and nightingales
when the reality of your existence
is finally accepted after years and years
when all this time you were really alive

a place where I see
six hundred and seventy-eight poets
with my first official glance from the slit between the curtains
six hundred and seventy-eight poets —
tricksters all! —who gad about in strange
beggar costumes digging around for rhyme,
for measure in piles of litter
and from the sound of my first official step
six hundred and seventy-eight occult nightingales
just for diversion's sake   took flight
from amidst turbid murky marshes, slick-slimed
six hundred and seventy-eight occult nightingales
disguised themselves as six hundred and seventy-eight
old black crows and flew lazily
towards the edge of day
and my first official breath
mingled with the perfume of six hundred and seventy-eight
rose branches produced by immense Plasco factories[2]

It's a gift, life is — in the birthplace of Sheikh
Abu Delqak, "Father of a Clown"[3]
the *kamanche* player and opium smoker,
ready to play any day.
it's a gift, life is — in the birthplace of Sheikh
"Baby, Baby —Do You Feel Alright? Alright!",
the lute-player of the Clan of Drummers —
and in the city of overweight stars
stars of thighs, hips, and tits and a little
art — these movie
stars displayed on magazine covers
it's a gift, life is — here in
the cradle of the authors of the philosophy
of "Hey, man! What's it to me? Forget it!"
here in the cradle of Olympic competition in intellect —
                                        OmyGawd!
here in the land where
whenever you touch a portable box
which blares out sounds and flashes images,

from that idiot box comes
the commotion of a fresh genius, a child prodigy
and here in the land where each one
of the self-chosen national thinkers,
when they attend adult classes, each one
of them is equipped — on their chests — with
six hundred and seventy-eight short order electric ovens
and on both hands they have
six hundred and seventy-eight "Navzer watches"[4]
arranged in rows and they know that
inability,
inability is the property
of empty-handedness not,
not of ignorance —
it's a gift, life is

I won. yes, I won.
now to celebrate this victory
I'll light six hundred and seventy-eight
candles — I bought them on credit
I light them proudly in front of the mirror
and I fly onto the top of the shelf to discourse,
if I may, if you would be so kind
as to hear me out, I'll discourse about
life's legal principles
and I lay into the crown
                        of my own head
with the pick-axe at the ground-breaking ceremony
of the high rise of my life — you know
one of those buildings — yeah, that's right
you got the picture, right
I'm bonging myself upside the head
while onlookers wildly applaud
I'm alive, yes alive like
the Living River, Zende Rood, which once was alive[5]
and I shall take a share in,
and benefit from, all the things
which are confined to living people

as of tomorrow I can stride
in the side streets and alleys of the city
which overflow with national donations,
shit,
and I can stroll among the carefree
shadows of telegraph poles
and six hundred and seventy-eight times
I can write with pride
lines of graffiti on the walls
of public toilet
stalls
I can write lines
that would make an ass laugh[6]

as of tomorrow I can hold dear in my heart
and mind, I can pursue
                    that great ideal
just like any zealous patriot—
pursue and take my share
of that great ideal which all that crowd
passionately and anxiously pursue:
every Wednesday afternoon I can have a share[7]
of those thousand nourishing thousand—
rial passions in my brain and body's frame[8]
those cash passions which can eat up
the expense of a refrigerator and furniture and curtains
or this prize money can be offered bribewise
to 678 male citizens one night
to buy off their own 678 naive votes

as of tomorrow I can do up some
right righteous stuff in the back room
                    of Khachik's shop.[9]
after snorting up a run of good nose-hits
off of several grams of un-cut pure white shit
and downing oh so many spiked glassfuls of Pepsi
and exclaiming "Oh, God"
        and "Oh, Sweet Lord" and

89

"quack-quack! Oh Lordie Oh sweet sweetie Lordie!"
and other such nonsense
and thereby having met the entrance
        requirements with these three actions,
as of tomorrow I can formally join in
the forum in Khachik's backroom
the forum of the learned academics and intellects
and the scholarly, liberal shit-heads
and the rabble and down-home followers of
"uhn-uhn, oh-oh, uhn-uhn, oh-oh, hey I feel alright!"
—all these kinds of faker fakirs in the forum!
and there in the forum of Khachik's backroom
I can draw up the plan for my first great novel
I'll sketch it out on both sides of the covers
of six hundred and seventy-eight packages
of original "Oshno Special" cigarettes [10]
ah! the plan for my first great novel
which will officially go to press —
                an empty-handed printing press—
along about the year one
        thousand six hundred and seventy-eight
according to the sun
calendar . . . the Sun of Tabriz [11]

as of tomorrow I can invite myself
with complete trust in myself
to the next congress of the panegyric club
or what's known as the "thank you" club
for six hundred and seventy-eight congressional terms
I can invite myself
to its auditorium with velvet-covered seats
because I keep up with the *Journal of Arts and Knowledge*
and I read flattery and homage
and because I know the forms
of "correct writing" and "correct speech."

I stepped into the arena of existence
I stepped amidst the creative heap,
heap of contenders, creators, and players

and this great arena of science and knowledge
has carried him in triumph to the threshold [12]
            of forging artificial clouds,
has won for him the unveiling, the revelation
                of neon lights— [13]
all this was accomplished, of course,
in the centers for experiment and research
at sales counters of roast chicken stands

I stepped into the arena of existence
I stepped into the pell-mell creative heap
although the heap doesn't have any bread,
instead of bread it does have wide
peripheral vision, an open view, a vast scope
of thought. Its present geographical boundaries are,
towards the north: Teer Square, lush [14]
freshness and wet green growth; to the south:
the creative heap shares the boundary
with the ancient E'daam Square; [15]
in areas full of overflowing throngs, the heap
extends to the Artillery Park. [16]

and in the sky's shining
asylum of security, its own security,
and in the sky's shining asylum
from morning to sunset's dark, six
hundred and seventy-eight solid
strapping plaster figures of swans, along
with six hundred and seventy-eight
angels — O what angels! — molded, kneaded
from clay and mud — all these
are occupied in propagating trademarks, [17]
trademarks of tranquility, silence and immovability

ii
I won. yes, I won
so long live number 678, resident
of Tehran, issued from the Fifth Ward

91

this card-holder has reached such exalted station
in the refuge of perseverance and determination
that number 678 has been established
in a window frame at the altitude of
678 meters above ground level

she has the honor and station
of this which
allows her to madly throw
herself out said same window,
hurtling head over heels and without benefit of steps, [18]
into the kind skirt of the Mommyland —

and her last
            will and testament is that
at the price of 678 coins
the honorable Mr. Abraham Sahba [19]
will write an elegy
in mish-mash haberdash rhyme
in eulogy of her life

I SHALL SALUTE THE SUN A SECOND TIME

I shall salute the sun
a second time
I shall greet the stream which coursed in me
a second time
I shall salute the clouds which were my prolix thoughts
a second time
I shall greet the painful growth of aspens
a second time
aspens of the garden which passed
through
dry seasons with me
a second time shall I

                              greet
                              flocks of crows
                    which used to bring me gifts
                    gifts of night-field smells
a second time shall I
greet
my
mother who lived in the mirror
          who was my old age's image
and again I'll greet
the earth, the burning innards of which,
my repeated lust used to cram with green
seeds   (for storage)
I'm coming   coming   I'm coming
with my hair   curls: continuance of underground
                    smells —
with my eyes: dense   experiences of darkness —
with the bushes which I've
clipped from the thickets on the other
                              side
                              of the wall
I'm coming   coming   I'm coming
and the doorway's threshold will
be filled   with love
and I'll greet them again — me
on the doorway — I'll greet
those who love and a girl still there
standing on the threshold full of love

YOU WERE KILLING ME

you were killing me
but you were my life
and I was dying due to you

you used to go with me
you used to sing in me
when I would wander aimlessly through
the avenues and streets
you would go with me
you would sing in me
amidst the elm trees you
used to invite sparrows in love
to the morning of the window.
when night would be drawn out and drag
on and on
when night would not end, then
amidst the elm trees you
would invite sparrows in love to
the morning of the window

you used to come to our street with your lights
you would come with your lights
when the kids would go
and when the groves of locust trees used to sleep
and when I remained alone in the mirror
you would come with your lights

you would grant your hands
you would grant your eyes
you would give
                   your kindness
when I was hungry
you would give your life
you were like light generous

you used to clip the tulips
and you would cover my hair curls
when my curls were trembling from nakedness
you would clip the tulips

you used to lay
your cheeks against the anxiety of my breasts

when I had nothing left
to say you would lay
your cheeks against the anxiety of my breasts
and you would listen
to my blood which flowed moaning
to my love crying as it was dying

you would listen
but you didn't
                        see me

A REBIRTH

i

all my existence is a dark sign a dark[1]
                        verse
that will take you by itself
again and again
through incantation of itself
over and over
to eternal dawn
                        bloomings and eternal growth
in this verse, in this sign
I sighed for you, sighed
in this verse, in this sign, I versified
you, I joined you
to tree and water and fire

ii

perhaps life
is a long avenue through
which a woman passes each day
with a basket
perhaps life is a rope
with which a man hangs

himself from a branch
perhaps life is a kid who
returns from school
life could be lighting up
a cigarette in the relaxing interval
between two
love-makings
                        or life
could be could be some confused
transit of a passerby
who takes
off his hat and to another passerby says
"good morning" with
a mean
            -ingless smile

perhaps life is that   stopped instant in which
my gaze lays waste to itself,
my gaze into the no-no of your eyes
self-destructs
                        and there is a sense in this
which I shall mix in with
comprehension of the moon
and with perception of the pitch dark.

in a room as large as one loneliness
my heart, as large as one love, beholds
the simple subterfuges of its happiness
        in the beautiful way the flowers in the vase fade
        in the sapling which you planted in our garden
        and in the song of canaries, which
        song is only as large as a window
. . .ah, this
is my share
this is my share
my share is a sky, which sky
will be taken from me by
                        hanging
                  a curtain over it

98

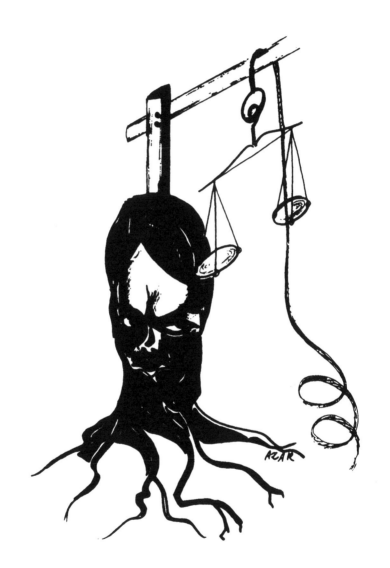

my share is to descend by
an abandoned stairwell and come   together
with something in rotteness and exile
my share is a grief-stained stroll in memory lane
        and giving up the ghost
        in the sorrow of a voice
        which calls to me, saying:
        "I love
        your hands."

I plant my hands in the garden
I shall grow green, I know I know I know
and swallows'll lay eggs
in deep cracks around my ink-
                        stained fingernails

I suspend earrings from my two
ears — earrings of two twin dark red cherries
and I'll paste dahlia leaves
                on my fingernails[2]
there is an alley where boys
who were in love with me — boys
with the same disheveled hair,
scrawny necks and stick-legs —
they dream of
a girl's innocent smiles
a girl who was carried away
one night by the wind

there is an alley
that my heart has stolen away
from my childhood's neighborhoods

the trip of a blob down the line of time
and said blob impregnating the dry line
                                of time
the blob of a conscious image which image
is reflected back from a party mirror

and it's this way
that somebody dies,
that somebody remains

iii
no hunting or fishing worth mentioning
in a piddling little old crick
which flows into a ditch
no pearls there for a fisherman to catch
I know a small sad mermaid
who lives
in an ocean and she
plays her heart
                gently, gently
on a wooden lip flute — list! . . .
a small sad mermaid
who dies in the night from one kiss
and she
will be born at daybreak
from one kiss

NOTES

TO I. G. (p. xiv, dedication)

1. "I. G." probably stands for Ibraham Golestan, short-story writer, author of *The Stream, Wall, and the Thirsty Man* and *Tide and Mist*.
2. Aayeh: This word originally means "sign" in Arabic, in the same sense that people were said to cry out to Jesus (see the Gospels): "Give us a sign [from God]!" Mohammed the Prophet considered each of the verses of his recited Message as a Sign. Hence, a verse of the Koran is called an "aayeh."

THOSE DAYS (p. 1)

1. Chador: woman's veil.
2. Nouruz: New Year's Holiday, from March 21 to April 2.
3. Messenger flowers: dandelions.

ON THE EARTH (ON THE GROUND) (p. 10)

1. These dots are integral parts of the letters like the dot in the English "i."

TRAVEL POEM (p. 13)

1. Aayeh-haa: see "TO I. G.", p. xiv, dedication, note 2.
2. As there may be no pictures, images, statues, *etc.* in any Muslim mosque by express command in the *Koran*, Muslim architects have inscribed aayeh-haa (*aayehs*) (signs, verses) of the *Koran* upon the walls of mosques. As for the Muslim, the *Koran* is the very *speech of God*; like the transformed host in the Catholic Mass for a Christian, a written verse of the *Koran* is direct evidence of God's existence and God's love for a Muslim.

GHAZAL (p. 16)

1. Ghazal: a type of rhymed and metered Persian poem usually on topics of love and sadness.
2. H. A. Saayeh is the pen name of Hooshang Ebtehaaj. It is curious that his pen name means "shadow" (saayeh) in Persian.
3. Here the poet is addressing the man's penis.
4. Forooq: light, brilliance. This is also the poet's name.
5. Saayeh: shadow. This is also the name of the man to whom this poem is dedicated. He is being addressed (as "you") in the next line. See note no. 1.

IN THE GREEN WATERS OF SUMMER (p. 17)

1. Inscriptions or bas-reliefs sculptures have been made in Iran at least since the time of the early Kassites, ca. 2200 B.C. The bas reliefs have mainly a royal cast in the main roles of the action depicted. The inscriptions are all royal inscriptions. The allusion here, if allusion were intended by the poet, is the passing of

the old order. For an analogous but weaker symbolic situation, imagine the presidential faces on Mount Rushmore falling down.
2. Alternate reading: "we tremble from dread of roaming lost." The version in the text proper would corroborate the allusion suggested in note 1.
3. Its own: "the Nothing's" own.

FORGIVE HER (p. 21)

1. "Oo": he, him; she, her. In Persian there is no differentiation of gender in the third person pronoun. Amin Banani suggests that this is in reference to the poet Ahmad Shaamloo who was an inspiration to Forooq during a poetic dry period, in which case the pronoun should read "he" or "him." Line 31, "down into the soil of his/her exile" would tend to corroborate Dr. Banani's view as Ahmad Shaamloo lived in exile from Iran in New Jersey and London. Nonetheless, the ambiguous use of the pronoun "oo" ("he/she" and "him/her"), used explicitly in this poem only in the objective sense (bar oo: on him/her), allows the poem to expand in meaning.

LOVINGLY (p. 27)

1. Rood: stringed instrument akin to the lute.

BARRIERS (p. 34)

1. *Mihrab*: this is a niche in a mosque indicating the direction of the Ka'ba in Mecca (*qibla*), the direction of prayer. Every mosque has at least one such (external) focus of worship. In Iran, the *mihrab* is always in this shape: ⌂ Also, it is usually recessed into the back wall.

THE MOON'S LONELINESS (p. 40)

1. Layla: legendary lover of Qays ("Majnoon": the madman) who went mad from the love whose consummation was blocked by Layla's father.
2. Purdah: harem; that portion of the house which is curtained off and is prohibited to males who are not members of the family. The word "purdah" ("pardeh" in Persian) itself means "curtain."
3. One might speculate that here the moon represents the late Shah of Iran, Muhammad Reza Pahlavi.

MY LOVE (p. 41)

1. Majnoon: mad, insane, possessed by jinn. This is the name of the most famous lover in the Muslim World, Qays of the Tribe of 'Aamery, called "Majnoon" because he went mad from his frustrated love for Layla. They were of two different tribes of the Arabian Desert. As their tribes were at war with each other, they could not marry. Another version has it that Majnoon's father inadvertently insulted Layla's father during marriage negotiations which broke down as a result, Layla's father forbidding such a marriage.

IN THE COLD STREETS OF NIGHT (p. 43)

1. This is probably a reference to the Muslim dawn call to prayer (*Īzāne-saḥar*).

BOG (p. 50)

1. Bog: "mordaab." Literally, this means "dead water."
2. Eye: eye of soul.
3. Kites: (figuratively) vultures.
4. "Its mate" (my eye's mate), "him".
5. Independence: "esteghnaa." This is a Sufi term for "needlessness" of anything except God.

EARTH SIGNS (p. 52)

1. Reference to Muhammed the Prophet when he was meditating in the cave outside Mecca. Later on he fled from the Meccans (Hejra) to that same cave with Abu Bakr ("Companion of the Cave").
2. This reminds one of the line by Sohrāb-e Sepehry:
   che edrākī az ta'm-e majhūl-e nān dar madhāq-e resālat taravīd
   the unknown flavor of bread on the palate –
   what import this message exudes! –
   prophecy is made of this.
   (From "*Be Bāgh-e Hamsafarān*": "To the Garden of Fellow Travellers" in *Hajm-e Sabz, The Extent of Green*, included in *Hasht Kitab*, p. 397).
   It is difficult to tell which poet influenced the other here, if there be influence, for the two poets were friends and familiar with each other's work. Besides, the two poems could have been written in approximately the same period (1962-63). My suspicion, however, is that in this case, Foroogh was reacting to Sohrāb.
3. Gilt leaves: reference to the *Koran*, the leaves of which are sometimes gilt.

NIGHT VISITATION (p. 58)

1. *Khodaa haafez*: This is the common parting salute which means literally, "God preserve you!", like the Arabic "(May you remain) in God's safety!" (*fee amaan illaah*), the French "Adieu" (to God), and the English "Godspeed."

CONQUEST OF THE GARDEN (p. 72)

1. "Merged with lamp and water and mirror": this is related to the *'aqd* ceremony with its stone-bread (*nān-e sangak*), flowers and white candy (*noql*) wherein a man and a woman are pledged to marry each other. A *mulla* (master of religious law) presides over the ceremony.
2. *Simurgh, seemorgh*: This enormous mythical bird of Iran is never seen except in various epic or mystical episodes in Persian literature. This "Bird of Knowledge" symbolizes both wisdom and Divine Unity. Generally it inhabits the upper reaches of Mount Qaf, the mythical World Mountain which lies at the center of the (flat world) of the ancient Arabic and Islamic Cultures. The one exception to this geographic location of the simurgh is the simurgh which

made its home on the upper slopes of Mount Damavand (near contemporary Tehran). To this simurgh was entrusted the orphaned Zal for education and upbringing according to Ferdowsi's *Epic of the Kings* (*Shah Nameh*). Zal was the father of Rostam. In another epic episode, Rostam was mortally wounded in battle by Esfandiyar, who like Achilles was invulnerable save for one part of his body, his eyes. The simurgh rescued Rostam, licked his wounds clean, curing him with his magic tongue, and in addition, instructed him in means of slaying Esfandiyar.

In Sohrawardi's mystical recital, "Reddish Mind" ("*Aql-e Sorkh*")— "L'Archange Empourpré .. in Henry Corbin's translation of Sohrawardi's mystical recitals under the same title—the simurgh is Divine Light or Universal Intelligence, the First Emanation from the (Neo-platonic) Whole. This simurgh was put to flight by the coming of the night (its nature is incompatible with darkness) and nightly thus abandoned Zal—Zal who in this version was first abandoned by his parents because his hair was pure white at birth. They took this as a sign that Zal was not of this world so they ostracized him in fear. Rostam killed Esfandiyar in this version by wearing polished armor in a location where Esfandiyar had to see a reflection of the simurgh off of Rostam's armor. Esfandiyar was dazzled to immobility by the sight of the simurgh (Pure Light) thus becoming vulnerable to Rostam's sword. The mystical intent of this passage is that Esfandiyar was annihilated (*fanā'*) in God by sight of God ("Sea of Light").

In *The Conference of the Birds*, 'Attar symbolized Divine Unity (*towheed*) with the simurgh. Normally in other stories of the simurgh, beholders of it see innumerable beautiful images and scenes on its feathers. However, for 'Attar, the thirty birds that finally attain to the vision of the simurgh, see only themselves *as the simurgh* (*si*: 30, *murgh* = bird[s]).

RED ROSE (p. 75)

1. It is said of the souls assembling on the vast square of the Judgment on Resurrection Day that they will be arrayed in ranks under a separate banner for each rank.

" 'ALI'S MOTHER SAID TO HIM ONE DAY ..." (p. 76)

1. From a children's poem taught in school:
   " 'Ali's mother said to him one day:
   'Beware! don't go near the pool!'
   He went and suddenly fell into the pool.
   Dear child—listen to your mother!"
2. A two-rial piece was roughtly equivalent to a nickel.
3. "Zero": bottom-most possible score in the Persian grading system. "Twenty" is the highest score. Hence a "two" marked in next to a zero would be a student's way of trying to make the worst score the best.
4. When a Persian Muslim makes a vow, special food is often cooked and eaten to mark the vow.
5. "Glow-pearl" (shab cheragh): a fabulous pearl radiating light at night like a lamp. It roughly corresponds to a "will o' the wisp."
6. The last two lines in this section come from a children's rhyme chanted by the kid who is "it" in "hide-and-go-seek":

   1 that family our house, may it not rain (Rashti variant of first
   2 two two Scotchy   three lines came from
   3 that and ours and house and soup   Russian in World War II.)

4   needles and scissors

. . .

1   ten twenty thirty
2   forty fifty sixty
3   seventy eighty ninety one hundred
4   now that "hundred's" been called
5   pick up the blue hanky
6   pick up hanky full of pears
7   hear ye ta ta
8   know ye . . .
9   stop at Hajji's house

Lines one through four are Russian-influenced and are nonsense rhymes in Persian. "Hajji": someone who has gone on the pilgrimmage to Mecca (hajj). Usually only rich people can afford to take the pilgrimmage, hence "Hajji" is also an epithet for a rich man. As far as I know, the title or epithet is never used for women in Iran.

7. "Wind catcher" (*bād gīr*): a structure constructed in the hot regions of Iran bordering on the great deserts to catch the cool winds and funnel them down to rooms underground.

8. In other words, "don't do anything which will make the *divs* (devils) in hell put your name on their blacklist and plague you with bad luck (and maybe damnation)!"

9. Blindness and baldness when they came before old age were a sign of being in the lower classes twenty years ago. There were two diseases in Iran, one which caused blindness (cataracts?—red eyes and squinting were the symptoms) and the other which caused premature baldness.

10. This is the shrine (*imāmzādeh*: progency of an imam) of Hazrat Abdol Azim ("slave of the One On High"), great-grandson of Imam Hassan the second Imam (spiritual link between the community and God) of the Shi'a Muslims. It is situated in Rayy, an ancient city just south of Tehran.

11. The first railroad in Iran ran from Tehran to Rayy.

12. Paamenaar: the oldest district in Tehran, just north of the bazaar, usually known by the name of Takieh Gah, Shams al-Amarra.

13. Takieh: Takieh Gah: mourning or passion theater of the martyrs, especially for Hossein, Third Imam and Prince of Martyrs. During the passion plays and parades of the month of Moharram ("prohibited"), the audience participates by smiting their breasts in rhythm and chanting a choral response to the dialogue being spoken on stage or being chanted by a parade leader.

14. This is possibly a reference to the miracle of Jesus with the fish and bread distributed to the hungry crowd on the shores of Lake Galilee.

15. This is a double reference. One Fatimah was the favorite daughter of the Prophet. She married 'Ali, the first Shi'ite Imam. The line in the poem refers to a common saying meaning "there isn't enough."

16. The second part of the double reference alluded to above is a reference to a famous whore, "Fatimah Elephant-Cunt." She had a miserly pimp (so the story goes) who gave her a small piece of cloth to make a pair of pants ("panties"). Of course there wasn't enough material to cover the enormous hip area of Fatimah Elephant-Cunt. Hence again, "there isn't enough." I have translated "tambun" as "panties" whereas they are actually long breeches worn under a skirt.

Notice the quick swerving from religious to secular references in this poem. Sometimes they are intermixed and combined (as in the line under discussion) reflecting the same intermixture in popular culture and speech.

17. Shishkebob with rice.

18. False-modesty (*nāmūs bāzī*): another possible translation would be "reputations." In kids' talk it means "fucking."

107

19. Chador: veil worn by Muslim women in Iran.
20. In the days of Reza Shah the Great (second quarter of this century), the folk were summoned to the artillery park (Tūp Khāneh) in Tehran where the great Army Square (Maidān-e Sepah) now stands, to watch the execution.
21. Agha Bata Khan: a famous and popular handsome young bandit of the late Qajar period. One of his relatives betrayed his place of hiding to the police. He was captued and shot. When the folk heard of this, many mourned for him.
    Notice the references to various kinds of martyrs in this poem. This is an ancient strain of Iranian culture stretching back perhaps three thousand years—at least to the Parthian Era (ca. 100 B.C.-A.D. 200) when the old heroic epic rounds were revived. Some scholars believe that the passion plays for the Shi'i Muslim Imam Hossein were first instituted for the slaying of Sohrab by his father Rostam, the warrior hero of the epic book *Book of Kings* (Ferdowsi), or for the murder of Siyavush, another prince in the Book of Kings.
22. These are the lines designating the end of a children's game somewhat like dodge-ball except that the "side" which is "free" can run wherever they choose within a given (bounded) large area. The "pursuers" must run after them and hit them with a ball (only one ball allowed). When all of one "side" is hit, the "pursuers" chant the ending lines. "In the name of God ...": short for "In the name of God, the Compassionate, the Giving." This verse heads every chapter (sura) of the *Koran*. It is used for all "starting" occasions, including, starting to eat, getting into a car, etc.

O LAND FULL OF JEWELS (p. 86)

1. This is in reference to the famous anthem which starts out: "O Iran! O land full of jewels!"
2. Plasco: the name of the great Iranian plastics manufacturing firm (PLAStics COmpany).
3. Sheikh Abu Delqak: "Sheikh" is a religious title so this would translate as something like "the Honorable Father of a Clown." He was an opium-smoking player of an instrument like a violin, the "kamanche" ("little bow"). These types generally haunt the streets in front of brothels and pimp on the side. With the sound of the word "kamanchekesh" (kamanche-player/little bow puller), the poet is alluding to the seedy, seamy side of this business. The word for "pimp" in Persian is "koskesh" (cunt-puller). The other musicians referred to in the text line also would generally pimp on the side.
4. Navzer: tradename of Samad Rezvan, watch manufacturer. (Spell the last name backwards to get "Navzer"). Here the poet is mocking the photo-graphic propensities of her countrymen/countrywomen who when posing for photos lean on their elbows like Rodin's sculpture, "The Thinker," while at the same time exposing their gold rings and gold watches to the camera. These rings and watches are supposed to indicate the level of their owners' education. "Navzer" was the best make of Irani watches at that time (ca. 1960).
5. Zende Rood: literally, the "Living River," the river which passes through the heart of Esfahan.
6. This is in reference to a couplet of poetry written by someone who had terrible penmanship: "I wrote a line which would make an ass laugh/the writer's cock goes up the ass of whomever reads it." The second line was altered in typical graffiti fashion to read, "The reader's cock goes up the writer's ass."

7. This is a reference to the national lottery once held every Wednesday afternoon. The proceeds of the lottery were supposed to go to charity, i.e., to be distributed by the government. When the time would draw close to the drawing held at the close of the day, you could hear the lottery-ticket hawkers yelling in the streets, "today! today!" as they waved the lottery tickets in your face. The highest prize at the time Foroogh was writing was a thousand one-thousand rial notes (1,000,000 R), or approximately $14,300.00.
8. Rial: unit of Irani currency once equivalent to 1.43 cents. A thousand rials was roughly equivalent to US $14.30.
9. Khachik: name of a famous liquor seller in Tehran.
10. These cigarettes have a sketch of Mt. Damavand (17,000+ feet) on the package cover. The paper is sufficiently clear and lightly colored for one to be able to write on both the inside and outside of the cover. The best tobacco in Iran is grown in Oshnavi-ye (in Kurdistan).
11. Shamsi Tabrizi: literally, "the Sun of Tabriz." He was Mowlaanaa Jalaal ad-Deen Roomi's (Our Lord the Divine Wrath of Religion, of Room—Rome—i.e., Turkey) spiritual guide or pir. Mowlaanaa (Roomi) named his monumental collection of short mystical poems after his pir who supposedly disappeared in a riot fomented by the folk of Roomi's adopted city Qonya against Shams himself. This immense volume by the most famous of mystical poets in the Muslim East contains perhaps the highest flights of spiritual ecstasy in Persian poetry.
12. Him: the former Shah of Iran, Mohammad Reza Pahlavi. There was a famous photo of the Shah waving his hand and appearing as if he were standing on clouds.
13. This is in reference to *Kashf al-Mahjoob* (*Revelation of the Veiled*), a famous Sufi manual of mysticism by Hujwiri.
14. Tir Square: "tir" means "gun, arrow, shot, bullet." At one time, this square was where political prisoners went up in front of the firing squad.
15. E'daam Square: literally, "Gallows Square" or "Execution Square."
16. Artillery Park (Toop Khaaneh): literally, "Cannon House." Its name was changed to Army Square (Maidan-e Sepah) during the time of the former Shah.
17. This is a reference to the Swan Trademark for vegetable oil of the Swan Oil Company. In recent times past, there was a neon sign visible from the Artillery Park (now Maidan-e Sepah) advertising this oil with a flashing neon swan. The blanket advertising of this product introduced the idea of cooking with vegetable oil (as versus animal fat which was traditionally used for cooking). Some concerned parties tried to stop the sale of this new oil by saying: 1) that it caused sexual impotence; 2) that it was used like vaseline for "unnatural" sexual intercourse; 3) by calling it "stink" instead of swan ("boo" instead of "qoo"); 4) by claiming that mice were found in it. This Swan Oil Co. was owned by Baha'is, a minority and somewhat despised sect in Iran, an offshoot of Islam. The Qajar laws making it a capital crime to be a Baha'i (or Babi, the earlier antecedent sect started by the Bab, the "Gate") have still not been repealed, hence Baha'is registered themselves as Muslims, Christians or whatever else. Under the present regime of Khomeini they have been openly persecuted.
Mommyland: "Mom-e Vatan," diminutive form of "Madar-e Vatan" (Motherland).
The honorable Mr. Abraham Sahba: A poet famous for occasional verses and elegies written in sing-song nonsense rhymes (literally, "curdled whey"). His name is really Ibrahim, but by using the foreign spelling, the poet mocks his foreign inclinations. "Honorable" was used as an honorific title for professors who didn't have a higher degree.

1. Aayeh: this word originally means sign in Arabic, in the same sense that people were said to cry out to Jesus (see the Gospels): "Give us a sign (from God)!" Mohammed the Prophet considered each of the verses of his recited Message as a Sign. Hence, a verse of the *Koran* is called an "aayeh."

2. Girls in Iran sometimes hook/hang cherries (with forked stems, the crotch of the stem being above the ear giving an upside down V-shape with the cherries at the two bottoms of the V) and paste dahlia leaves on their fingernails as the first kind of makeup. This is of course before they get to the age where they feel they can buy and wear commercial makeup.

EPILOGUE

LET'S BRING FAITH
TO THE ONSET OF THE COLD SEASON

and this is me
a lone and lonely woman
at the threshold of a cold season
at the beginning of understanding earth's stained being
    and of understanding
    pure and simple despair
    and of understanding
    the sky's overcast and cloudy melancholy
    and these cement hands' impotence
time passed
time passed and the clock struck
four, struck four, struck four, struck four
today's date is December 21st, the first
day of winter
I know the secret of the seasons
and I comprehend the speech of moments
the savior has gone to sleep in the grave
and the earth, the accepting receiving earth
is a sign of peace

time passed and the clock struck four.
wind blows cold down the alley
wind blows cold down the alley
and I am thinking about the love-mating,
    trellis-making of flowers—
    about buds with anemic stalks
    and about this consumptive wasted age
    and a man passing between damp trees—
    a man whose blue cords of veins
    have crawled up both sides of his throat
    like dead snakes.
    on the disturbed temples of his head
    that bloody scorning syllable is repeated:
    "peace"
    "peace"[1]
and I am thinking about the love-mating,
    trellis-making of flowers

113

at the threshold of a cold season
and where mirrors assemble to mourn
and where the society of pale experiences and mourners gathers
at this sunset pregnant with silent knowledge
how can that person keep on going this way:
patiently
   heavily
confused and aimlessly wandering?
the command was given: "halt!"
how can it be said of a man
that he isn't alive,
he has never been alive?

wind blows cold down the alley.
in old languid gardens, individual
crows were circling, solitary and aloof,
and the ladder's height is so trifling

they plundered the entire simplicity of a heart
and carried it off with them
to the castle of fables.
and now, how
will a body ever again
be able to rise to dance?
and how will she ever again
be able to dangle her childish hair in flowing waters?
and now, how will she ever again
be able to stomp underfoot the apple
which has finally been picked and smelled? [2]

my love, O my most matchless love!
how black are the clouds waiting
for the feast day of the sun!

perhaps it was by embodying flight
that that bird appeared one day
on the wing in the airlanes

perhaps those fresh leaves which breathed
in the lust of the breeze—
perhaps they emerged from dream's green lines
perhaps
that violet flame which burned
in the windows' clear mind
was just an innocent fancy of the lamp

wind blows cold down the alley
this is the beginning of utter ruin
the wind was also blowing on that day
when your hands were laid waste.
when dear stars, dear pasteboard stars
are in the sky, lies
begin to blow in the wind
how can she ever again
take refuge in the disgraced *sooras* of the prophets? [3]
we will be thrown together
like the millions of millenial dead
and then the sun will cast judgment
upon the corruption of our corpses
I'm cold
I'm cold and perhaps I'll never be warm again
my love, O my most matchless love!—
"How old was that wine?
It really did a job on us, didn't it?"
look how heavy time weighs on us!
and look how fish chew my flesh!
why do you always hold me down
                        on the ocean floor?

I'm cold and I've had it
with mother of pearl earrings—
I loathe those "mothers"
I'm cold and I know
that nothing will remain
of the entirety of red surd dreads
of one wild anemone
except several bloodrops in red

I'll free all the lines from their rigid tracks
likewise I'll liberate the counting of numbers
I'll take refuge from the circumscribed limits
of closed geometrical figures and seek
asylum in the wide open spaces
of a sense of vastness and expanses
bare I am, bare, bare, I am bare
like the silences between words of love
                    I am stripped bare
and all my wounds bleed freely from love
from love, love, love.
I have passed beyond
this wandering confused island
by way of ocean's roiling turmoil
                    and by volcanic eruption
and shattering fragmentation: disintegration
was the secret of that integrated existence,
the sun being born from
its most insignificant atom

hello innocent night!   peace!
peace to you O night which converts the eyes
of desert wolves to bone marrows of faith and open trust.
beside your water channels, O innocent night
the spirits of willows smell
the spirits of kind axes
I come from the world where
thoughts, letters, and sounds are
                    undifferentiated
and this world is like a nest of vipers
and this world is full with sounds of people's
moving hurrying footsteps, people who
weave your hanging noose while they kiss you

hello, innocent night!   peace!

there's always some distance, an interval,
between window and seeing.
why didn't I look? —

116

like that time when a man passed
between damp trees
I didn't look

why didn't I look?
perhaps my mother cried that night
that night I arrived
to pain and was conceived
that night I was made bride to acacia clusters
that night Isfahan was filled with the tinkling of blue
tiles, and that person who was half of me
had come back inside
                    my foetus
I would see him in the mirror
he was bright clean clear like a mirror
suddenly he called me
and I was made bride to acacia sprays
perhaps my mother cried that night.
what a fuile useless brightness that was
which rebelled in the closed confines of this opening—
this opening which was really a plugged-up hole.
why didn't I look?
all the happy moments knew all along
that your hands would be wrecked
and I didn't look
until the moment when the window of time opened
and that sad cuckoo chirped four,
announcing the hour of four
o'clock
          struck struck struck struck
and I ran into that little woman
whose eyes were like empty nests of simorghs[4]
and she used to move her thighs like so—
really getting into moving and letting go with the flow—
perhaps she carried off my glorious virgin dream
with her to night's bed

will I ever comb my hair in the wind again?
will I ever plant violet gardens again?

and will I ever set up geraniums
in the sky behind the window?
will I ever dance on glasses again?
will the doorbell ever carry me away again
        in expectation of a familiar voice?

I told my mother: "it's all over now."
I said: "you always thought it would happen.
we must send an obituary notice to the paper."

hollow people
trusting, hollow people—
their emptiness filled with confidence
look how their teeth
sign anthems when they chew
and look how their eyes
rip and devour when they open up wide
and how he passes between damp trees:
        patiently
        heavily
        confused and
        aimlessly wandering

at four o'clock
in moments during which the blue
cords of his veins crawled
up both sides of his throat like dead snakes
and on the disturbed temples of his head
that bloody scorning syllable is repeated:
        "peace!"
        "peace!"[1]
have you never smelled
that blue Marvel of Peru, that Flower of Four O'Clock

time passed
time passed and night fell
upon the bare acacia branches
night slipped behind the window panes
and sipped in the last dregs of the day

already passed away
with its cold tongue

where do I come from?
where do I come from?
. . .that I be so smeared with night's smell?
the earth is still fresh over his grave—
I mean the grave of those two
                                    young green hands . . .

how radiantly kind you were, my love,
O my most matchless love!
how kind you were when you lied!
how kind you were when you closed
the eyelids of mirrors, and when
you uprooted lustrous candles from silver candelabra
and when you carried me to love's pasture
in the oppressive murky dark, carried me
until that dizzy and curling smouldering smoke,
which was all that was left of thirst's blaze,
would lie down in sleep's meadow

and those pasteboard stars
endlessly circle around infinity.
why did they speak out loud?
why did they invite a glance
          as guest to the house of sight and vision
          and let it lodge there while it visits?
why did they carry away her caresses
          to the shame of her maidenhood's tresses?
look how that person's life is hung and executed
          up on the pole of dread fear and suspicion!—
that person who spoke with words
          who caressed with a look
          who soothed terror-struck shock with a caress
look how the marks of the five
          branches of your fingers that were like five
          letters of truth
          remain on her cheek!

what? what is silence, my matchless love?
what is silence but unspoken words?
I have to stick to words, but the speech of sparrows
is the live language of flowing sentences in nature's festival
the language of sparrows means: spring, leaves, spring
the language of sparrows means: breeze, scent, breeze
the language of sparrows dies in factories

who is this who wends her way
on eternity's highway towards moments of unity?
and she winds her eternal watch
with the mathematical logic of differentiations
who is this who doesn't know the cock's crow
for the start of the day's heart? —who knows
it rather for the smell of breakfast cooking?
who is this who wears love's crown? —
and who has rotted away amidst wedding gowns?

so then finally the sun in one
single instant of time didn't shine
on either pole of arctic despair
you were emptied by the tinkle of blue glazed tiles

and I, I am so full that they pray
when they hear the call in my lines

.
happy funerals
sad funerals
quiet meditative funerals
dressy funerals with pleasant encounters and good food.
how upset people get—in spots
where defined and bounded time stops,
and in uncertain areas of fleeting lights
          and buying-lust for spoiled fruits of pointlessness—
ah! how upset people get at accidents at intersections
and at shrills of whistles suddenly broken off
in moments during which a man must be, must be, must be

squashed under the wheels of time—
a man who passes between damp trees . . .

where do I come from?

I told my mother: "it's all over now."
I said: "you always thought it would happen,
I mean, some accident.
we must send an obituary notice to the paper."

hello O lonely alienation
I surrender
             the room to you
why are dark clouds always prophets
of fresh signs and new sacred verses
             of purification and sanctification?
and in the martyrdom of a candle
there is a brilliant mystery
which that last and most drawn-out
flame knows, well knows.

let's bring faith
let's bring faith to the onset of the cold
                                    season
let's bring faith to the ruins of dream
                           gardens—
         to idle sickles carelessly laid aside—
         and to prison grains and prison seeds
look how it snows . . .

perhaps those two young hands were the truth,
those two hands of the youth
that were buried under their load of snow,
snow which wouldn't let up, a blizzard unloosed.
and next year, when spring makes love
to the sky behind the window,
throbbing and pulsing in its vernal body
bubbling and boiling merrily away,

green fountains of light-weight stems will gush
and bloom into flower, my love,
O my most matchless love

let's bring faith to the onset of the cold

*

1. Peace: also, "hello."
2. Compare this despondent tone with the victorious tone of "we picked the apple" (*sīb rā chīdīm*) in "Conquest of the Garden," above, p. 72.
3. *Soora*: chapter of the *Koran*.
4. See note 2 of "Conquest of the Garden," p. 105, above.

FORMATION, CONFRONTATION, AND EMANCIPATION
IN THE POETRY OF FOROOGH FARRAKHZAAD

By Farzaneh Milani

The ties between women and poetry are deep and strong in Iran. Ever since the minstrelsy tradition and especially after the revival of the Persian language in the ninth century A.D., women have continuously contributed to the development of this poetry. Many women—far more than is commonly recognized—turned to poetry to exercise capacities otherwise frustrated by social restrictions.[1] Certainly, the suitability of this field as a creative outlet can be partly explained by the simple and practical fact that poetry is not only a more thoroughly integrated part of Persian's daily life, it can also be pursued in the privacy of home.

Literary criticism in Iran, however, has long possessed an overwhelmingly masculine character. A tradition of male making and of male concerns, it has responded rarely to the creativity of those women with ardent and sensitive souls. In fact, the pages of Persian literary history are filled not only with contributions of many unacknowledged poets but also with painful silences—silences that speak of the systematic attrition of female literary talent. Major studies of poetry deal almost exclusively with the work of men. The enormous gap between the time, space, and quality of attention devoted to male poets and that devoted to female poets is profoundly disturbing.

Only a small group of women have managed to elude oblivion, their works unduly patronized or inadvertently misunderstood. A sampling of the dominant critical trends in the readings of women's poetry points up several misconceptions, sexually biased assumptions, and a deliberate refusal to confront this poetry on its own terms, that is, as work that has been written out of the available experiences of a woman. More destructive, yet, has been the presentation of the few who survived and flourished as exceptions, unusual phenomena. Foroogh Farrokhzaad

---

[1] Keshavarz Sadr in *From Rabée to Parvin,* one of the very few books completely dedicated to women poets, refers to the valuable contribution of more than 100 women to Persian poetry and calls attention to the indispensability of retrieval and revival of their undervalued and neglected works: "Historians have written, to some extent, about male poets. Unfortunately, however, they have neglected the works and biographies of female poets. That is why the number of women poets must be quite different from the actual number of those who wrote poetry. It is indeed this very nonchalance and indifference that complicates the study of the life and poetry of women poets." (Teheran: Kavian Publishing, 1335/1956, p. 31).

is an eloquent case in point. Although unlike many others, she is not the kind of woman poet who needs to be unearthed and revived; although her work has never been plagued by neglect; yet, the nature of most of the criticism of her poetry leaves much to be desired.

Foroogh not only had the audacity to express explicitly her unorthodox convictions in poetry, but also the tenacity to act them out in life.[2] Quite simply, as she refused to be typecast in her work, she challenged and rejected accepted mores and assumptions about the conventional definitions of womanhood in life. An iconoclast, she ventured into forbidden fields in both life and literature and trespassed beyond the territory allotted to women. She thus enraged (and continues to enrage) guardians of high morality turned into critics. Indeed, the attacks on the "immorality" of her poetry are bland in comparison with the harsh criticism bestowed upon her personal life, criticisms which often seem to confuse one with another.

Farrokhzaad was both a woman conscious of her femaleness and a poet. "If my poetry, as you mentioned, has a certain air of femininity," she told interviewer Iraj Ghorghin, "it is obviously due to my being a woman. Fortunately, I am a woman."[3] Indeed, her whole body of work, since its earliest publication, bears her individuality of voice as a woman.[4] Without making gender her destiny, she wrote with an awareness that she was a member of a non-male tradition, making it difficult not to approach her poetry on its own terms. Part of the importance and magnetism of this work is that it allows the integration of a woman-self with poetry and refused to accommodate itself to dominant literary standards—the most insidious form of censorship.

Throughout her short literary career, Foroogh worked mainly in an atmosphere of denunciation and reproach from many critics.[5] However,

[2] With characteristic candor, Foroogh told interviewers Saedi and Tahbaz: "I believe in being a poet in all moments of life. Being a poet means being human. I know some whose daily behavior has nothing to do with their poetry. In other words, they are only poets when they write poetry. Then it is finished and they turn into greedy, indulgent, oppressive, short-sighted, miserable, and envious people. Well, I cannot believe their words. I value the realities of life and when I find these gentlemen making fists and claims—that is, in their poems and articles—I get disgusted . . . " (*Some Words with Foroogh*, Teheran: Morvari Publishing, 1335/1976, p. 79).

[3] Iraj Gorghin, "An Interview with Foroogh Farrokhzaad," *Arash*, ed. Syrus Tahbaz (Teheran: Darakhshan Publishing Co., 1345/1966), p. 33.

[4] Obviously, recognition of the necessity to consider the fact of sex in evaluating her poetry should not be construed as an attempt to place her in a special category among poets in general. Undoubtedly, she is one of the foremost Iranian poets in spite (and because) of her gender.

[5] It should be noted that there is a near absence of female critics from the long

avid and enthusiastic readers offered her their faithful and ceaseless support. In the words of Faridoun Guilani: "*The Captive, The Wall*, and *Rebellion*, which contain weak and most often trivial poems, sell out like hot cakes."[6] Critics were baffled by the enormous appeal of these books and rarely did they bother to investigate further their unusual allure and attraction.[7]

Perhaps what commands both attention and admiration among readers has something to do with the emergence of a significant poetic female character whose complexities defy easy categorization. Perhaps the continuously rewoven webs of passion and love depicted in these poems provide a cathartic release for what voluptuousness offers and puritanical morality withholds from many of her readers. In short, perhaps by its simultaneous portrayal of the thrill of being fetterless and free and the anxiety and uncertainty attached to it, it eloquently speaks of a confusion which in many of her readers, has remained silent. Indeed, far from being a history of trivialities, this poetry is an accurate observation of the real and unadulterated realm of womanhood, so often distorted in Persian literature.

The collection of Foroogh's poetry celebrates diversity—diversity of form, content, and concern. Evolution is the hallmark of the character of these poems. In fact, her work can be divided into three distinct parts, the first of which consists of poems published in *The Captive*. Although written by an unconventional woman, these poems fit readily into the category of "feminine" poetry. By feminine poetry, I mean poems written from the perspectives and out of the available experiences of a woman who has internalized her "femininity." Second, *The Wall* and *Rebellion* are "feminist" outcries. Here, the poet reacts bitterly and with sarcasm—a

---

list of reviewers of her poetry. *Javedaneh*, a collection of critical studies and poems on Foroogh, includes only three essays by women. Two are the rather intimate recollections of a sister and a friend. The third is a short commentary (almost a page), by another contemporary women poet, more in the nature of a eulogy than a critical analysis.

[6] Reza Barahani, a prominent literary critic, attributes this popularity to two major factors—the "sentimental" nature of her verses and the "lyrical" tastes of her readership. "The general public recognizes Foroogh through *The Captive, The Wall*, and *Rebellion*. And since their poetic consciousness has not reached a relatively high level of sensibility, they believe poetry means sentimentalizing about death, lover, God, husband, or child, . . . Furthermore, the mentality of the Persian people is lyrical. They attach a higher importance to lyrics and odes than to any other genre of poetry." (*Neghin*, No. 44, p. 16). However, the most immediate lure of Foroogh's poetry proves to be neither its "sentimentality" nor its "lyricism." Critically acclaimed Persian poetry abounds in both categories.

[7] Faridoun, Guilani, "Foroogh-advertisement+herlself," *Teheran Keyhan*, 10 February 1977, p. 2.

sarcasm that grows ever more barbed–to the tight fetters to which a woman has to submit. And finally, in *A Rebirth* and poems published posthumously, she emerges as a "female" poet, one who has left behind her earlier sense of victimization and anger and has found a new style of both living and writing.[8]

I do not intend to imply that all of Foroogh's poetry conveniently fits into one or another of the three categories suggested. These are merely general divisions, sometimes overlapping, and aspects of more than one can be seen in a single poem or period. However, since it has been repeatedly maintained by critics that *A Rebirth* can be considered as a total transformation in the life of the poet, a kind of miracle, the isolation of phases of intense crisis and growth will help refute such a misconception. The organizing principle behind the categories suggested is the belief that the poet experienced significant and conflict-ridden periods of change and adjustment. The richness and profundity of later writings grow directly out of the development of the poet's consciousness as a woman and as a poet. The first three collections provide the key to her development, the soil from which later work grows.

The Captive is a detailed rendering of the state of alienation of a woman torn between social and moral proprieties, (as defined by the dominant masculine culture,) and personal standards. It is the story of a woman who relentlessly resists uncritical adherence to restrictive codes of behavior and sexual confinement and yet is manipulated by a subtle internalization of cultural expectations and demands. There is thus an acute tension between the poet's perception of freedom and her internalized value system. She can neither deny herself freedom from culturally enforced sex-role restrictions nor can she liberate herself from the norm her society has taught her is the prerequisite for self-respect and morality. A few lines of the poem titled, "Promiscuous," portrays the severe feelings of guilt and the conflicts to which she is subjected:

[8] Elaine Showalter in her admirable study of women novelsts from 1800 to the present contends that all literary subcultures go through three major stages of development: first a phase of imitation and internalization (feminine); next a phase of protest (feminist); and finally a phase of self-discovery (female). *A Literature of Their Own: British Women Novelists from Bronte to Lessing.* (Princeton: Princeton University Press, 1977.) Frantz Fanon along with many others believes that the art of the colonized goes through the same three stages of imitation, exorcism, and liberation. Van Gennep in *Rites of Passage* suggests the same threefold classification for the rituals attached to the transitional states in a human life; these stages are devices necessary for the assimilation of an individual into new status. According to him, rites of passage follow three major phases of separation (from the old), transition, and incorporation (a rebirth into the new group or society with a new status).

Leave me, I am distressing,
unstable, frail, and sinning.
In my breast beats a foolish heart,
in that heart a thousand lusts.[9]

The poet of *The Captive* is disturbed and yet directed by her discontentment with roles traditionally assigned to women. She is frightened and yet fascinated by the flowering in her passions. She is tuned to and yet tormented by romanticized expectations. In short, she is a young woman who has a hard time forging an identity for herself. She thus shuttles back and forth between two sets of values, the society's and her own, unable to make peace with either or to integrate the two. A few lines of the title poem of the book best captures this feeling of entrapment, despair, and doubt:

It's you I desire, knowing I shall never
hold you long enough to satisfy my heart
That limpid sky is what you are
I in this corner, a bird caged apart

My famished eyes are gazing at your face
from behind these bars so cold and dark
I pray for some hand to approach me
when towards you on wings I would dart

I wait for that one careless instant
From this dark prison to be winging away
and laughing in the keeper's face
At your side my life beginning its new day

I think of this knowing I shall never
be able to escape this plight
For even if the keeper should let me go
I've lost all my strength for the flight[10]

Following the publication of *The Captive*, Foroogh leaves her husband and loses forever the custody of her only child (a pain which will bitterly agonize her to her last days). Ready to transgress beyond domestic morality, she deliberately refuses to be fixed in images or roles she does not find to her liking. Although in *The Wall* and *Rebellion* the poet continues to

[9] Foroogh Farrokhzaad. *The Captive* (Teheran: Amir Kabir, 1354/1975), p. 29.
[10] *Bride of Acacias.* Selected Poems of Foroogh Farrokhzaad. translated by Jascha Kessler with Amin Banani (New York: Caravan Press, 1982), p. 123.

be caught between pressures to conform and urges to confront; although a revised order of convictions and commitments clash head on with her traditional values; yet, with these continuing conflicts comes a much stronger and more sustained sense of autonomy.

Foroogh now experiences a different kind of dilemma. The unequal treatment of men and women attracts both her attention and anger. If in *The Captive* she chronicled mainly the restrictive experiences of a woman with the least amount of analysis, she now no longer views women's limitations as natural or inevitable. If earlier, she frantically and erratically sought transformation, she now depicts it. The very titles of both books capture their dominant mood of rebelliousness. Indeed, they both document the resentment of a woman who senses bitterly and actively her society's injustice against women. Here, men are presented as oppressors, responsible for a good deal of women's subjugation. Here, anger and revolt simmer with painful urgency and prove to be the inspiring force behind many poems. The poet has moved beyond the earlier revelation of a personal sense of confinement and expresses a wide range of social frustration.

> When your innocent eyes peruse
> this tangled book with no beginning,
> at the heart of every song you'll see
> the deeprooted revolt of ages blossoming
>
> There are no stars shining here
> the angels here are weeping, every one
> here the flower of the amaryllis
> is worth less than the desert thorn
>
> . . . .
> I've abandoned the shore of a spotless name
> In my breast there's the star of the storm—
> the gloomy space of my cell, alas,
> where my anger burns in its whirling room [11]

Although the released energy of the unattached woman is formidable in *The Wall* and *Rebellion*, a certain ambivalence still manifests itself in many poems. It is in the poem titled "Life," *Rebellion's* last poem, that the previous fearful attitude toward experience is replaced by a new, vigorous ability to respond to life. Even if the potential for conflicts has not quite disappeared from this poem, one feels the overwhelming experience of it has. Openness to experience is no longer viewed as a menace but as a delight. Every line of this poem reverberates with a kind of

[11] Ibid., p. 133.

vigorous capacity for living. A sense of triumph and psychic integration governs it:

> I am in love, in love with morning star
> in love with vagrant clouds
> in love with rainy days
> in love with whatever has your name on it
> I absorb with all my thirsty being
> the fervent blood of your every moment
> I so thoroughly gratify myself with you
> that I'll enrage your God![12]

By dissembling her anger in *The Wall* and *Rebellion* Foroogh succeeds in releasing herself from repression. This recogition of and contact with her anger although a step forward for the poet who can finally come to face directly the rage and discontentment she had suffered previously, is soon replaced by a more heightened and balanced perception. Foroogh herself describes both books as "a desperate exertion between two different stages of life; the last pantings before some kind of liberation."[13] Indeed, preoccupations shift in *A Rebirth* and a different kind of poetry develops. Concern moves from the personal to the collective, from the feminine to the human.

A Rebirth and poems published posthumously attest to a mature emotional richness. The poet's inner journey coupled with outer mobility equips her with the insight necessary to ascertain the real self, redefine her role, and discover new dimensions of experience. With the intimate and the personal as an ever-present background, the last two collections are indeed far removed from the predominantly personal (although by implication female) concerns of the first three collections. The degree to which Foroogh changes in her later writings becomes clear when one compares two dream poems. "Dream" from *The Wall* fantasizes the happy arrival of a Prince who will carry on his galloping horse the dreamer to a happily-ever-after land.

> Certainly, from a distant land
> a proud Prince will arrive
> his clothing of gold
> his chest hidden beneath pearls and jewels
> the hoofs of his galloping horse
> will dart on the city's pavement

---

[12] Foroogh Farrokhzaad. *Rebellion* (Teheran: Amir Kabir, 1355/1976), p. 136.
[13] M. Azad, "An Interview with Foroogh Farrokhzaad," *Arash*, p. 39.

flames of the sun will shine
on his beautiful crown . . . .
Suddenly a knock fills the house
towards it, on wings I dart
it is he. Yes! It is he.
"Oh, you Prince, you magic lover,
every night I dream of your arrival . . . " [14]

The dreamt-of-lover never shows up. Clearly not. And soon, confronting the disillusionment of her lulling reveries, Foroogh realizes that expectations have less validity than experience. Prince Charming will not be carrying her off and she has to settle for some not so heavenly terrestrial paradise. In "One Like No Other," from *Let's Bring Faith to the Onset of the Cold Season*, a wholly different range of aspirations and desires emerges—less fanciful and more literal. The savior no longer has a personal mission. His arrival has a collective significance:

Someone's coming
someone's coming
someone who is with us in his heart, in his breath,
in his voice

Someone whose coming cannot be arrested
and handcuffed, and thrown in jail

Someone amidst firecrackers from the sky above
Toopkhaneh Square will come and spread the tablecloth
and he will distribute the bread
and he will distribute the Pepsi
and he will distribute the public park
and he will distribute the whooping cough syrup [15]

Although a more intense sense of political consciousness coupled with a more cohesive vision differentiates the last two collections from the first three, the most significant aspect of *A Rebirth* remains the birth of a new protean self, revelling in a plethora of tantalizing options. It chronicles personal and artistic growth. It is the testimony of a new adventure in both art and life, a record of the struggle of a warrior who fought for every piece of her share of freedom.

In these poems, much more than in previous collections, personal

[14] Foroogh Farrokhzaad, *The Wall* (Teheran: Amir Kabir, 1955/1967), p. 20.
[15] Foroogh Farrokhzad, *Let's Bring Faith to the Onset of the Cold Season* (Teheran: Morvarid Publishing, 1353/1974), p. 70.

morality is discovered rather than assumed. If earlier the accepted pattern of interdependency of men and women was experienced and depicted, now it is rejected in favor of a more gratifying relationship—meaningful and regenerative. Indeed, Foroogh proves to be one of the exceptionally few writers throughout Persian literature to illustrate that many erotic, emotional, and intellectual possibilities lie outside the traditional feminine roles of marriage and motherood (woman's only codified and sanctified relationships in literature as in society). In short, this later poetry traces the emergence of a new female character who departs radically from the roster of feminine stereotypes. Her presence—vital and visible—refuses to pale away into prescribed roles or a background figure. With her reverent openness before life as before love and lust, she portrays the eventual, however agonized, triumph of a woman and an artist in discovering individuality.

This gradual shift in sensibility urges the poet to search for a new formal structure corresponding to her new perception of self and world. In need of new avenues of expression, Foroogh reaches a point where her poetic impulses can no longer be limited within traditional boundaries. The breadth of the content requires new words and imagery. The artist's developing skill in the manipulation of her materials is congruent—and unavoidably so—with a radical modification of meter. Regularity of line length and of strophic organization is thus abandoned in favor of a free-flowing structure.

Foroogh's new-found technical and imaginative power should be viewed as closely linked to the growth of a woman who wants to transcend traditional limitations both within herself and her art. Although in the 1950's, at the time she was writing her first poems, the modernistic poetic movement was gaining prominence in Iran, Foroogh continued to write traditional verse. A sense of restlessness with classical poetics permeates only a few poems in the first three collections. Of the eighty-six poems of *The Captive*, *The Wall*, and *Rebellion* only twelve lack consistent rhyming couplets and a clear adherence to classical formal tradition. This early writing is distinguished from more traditional verse only by the sheer novelty of its subject matter. The unconventionality of the content is in sharp contrast with the conventionality of the craft. Indeed, if the hallmark of later poems is freedom from traditional rules of versification through the development of the poetic personae, the ingenuity of the early poetry lies in the poet's skill in harnessing for her own purposes the form and techniques of traditional poetry.

A Rebirth and posthumous poems attest to long years of formal confrontation with language, a diligent practice of the craft coupled with years of reflection and inner unfolding. Submerged or only implied in her earlier poetry, her feelings and aspirations achieve explicit and eloquent expression in her later writings. In an interview with M. Azad, Foroogh claimed that her self-knowledge led ultimately to the coalescence of her formal and thematic pattern:

> If you believe that the problem of form is solved in my poems or that some kind of harmony governs their component parts, I take that to be the result of my achieving a level of fastidiousness, a general kind of selection, and not only at the time of creation. One has to begin from the first grade, get to the twelfth, and graduate.[16]

Losing sight of this ceaseless growth in Foroogh's poetry, many critics have lodged the influence of Ibrahim Golestan–Foroogh's companion and lover for the last eight years of her life–at the center of her development. Sadr-e-din Elahi repeats a dominant view, however poorly formulated, when he claims that:

> One can say that Faroogh was a still and feminine pond with no wave and no mobility. Ibrahim [Golestan], like a luminous stone, fell into that water and replaced the deadly calm and quiescence with lively stirring and dynamism.[17]

Never was Foroogh a feminine pond (do ponds have a sex too?) suffering from inertness and inactivity. On the contrary, throughout her writing she assumes responsibility for an ever-changing self. From first to last, her poems clearly portray her resentment of stagnation in a "pond with no wave and no mobility."[18] Fixation on her relations with men, especially with Golestan, rather than attention to her evolving journey of self-discovery reveals the limited boundaries imposed by critics on her sexual roles and relationships.

[16]*Azad*, Arash, p. 44.

[17]Amir Esmaili and Abol-ghasem Sedarat, eds. *Javedaneh*. (Teheran: Marjan Publishing, 1345/1966), p. 83.

[18]It is interesting to note that the image of standing water and swamp recur frequently in Foroogh's poetry and always with negative connotations (see for instance "Bog"). Moving water, on the other hand, has positive application throughout her poetry. In the poem titled "To Ali Said his Mom, one Day ... " Ali has to decide between two alternative life styles. He can choose a secure, safe, and quiescent life. Or, he can lead a life of adventures, dangers, and mobility, represented by the sea. Ali moves out of the protective circle to search for wholeness and integration of self— metaphorically he joins the water, the sea.

The canon of Foroogh's work makes up a passionate autobiographical statement which gradually unfolds to become much more, to take in the concerns of a whole generation of women (and even a society) that was struggling—both personally and collectively—for (self) acceptance outside of traditional mores. The honesty and intimacy with which this struggle emerges, the vibrancy of the poet's life along with the zestfulness of her commitments—both as a woman and as an artist—set her poetry apart from most of Persian poetry. Although Foroogh's sense of a woman's rightful place both in her own regard and that of her society reaches its full flowering in later poems, each of her five collections in its own way presents an increment of that slow blossoming. Not long before she died, Foroogh wrote:

> I am glad my hair has turned grey, grooves have appeared on my forehead, and between my eyebrows two large wrinkles have settled. I am glad I am no longer fanciful and romantic. Soon I'll be thirty-two years old. Although being thirty-two means to have consumed so much of my share of life, in return I've found myself. [19]

The satisfactions of this quest were not to be enjoyed for long, and the journey was to be ended too abruptly. On February 14, 1967, at the very height of her poetic career, Foroogh died in an automobile accident.

[19] Azad, *Arash*, p. 5.

133

فروغ فرخزاد

تولدی دیگر

و برگزیدهٔ اشعار

غزل

ای مرز پرگهر

ایمان بیاوریم به آغاز فصل سرد

آیه های زمینی

عاشقانه

MAZDA PUBLISHERS

تولدی دیگر

همهٔ هستی من آیهٔ تاریکیست
که ترا در خود تکرارکنان
به سحرگاه شکفتن‌ها و رستن‌های ابدی خواهد برد
من در این آیه ترا آه کشیدم، آه
من دراین آیه ترا
به درخت و آب و آتش پیوند زدم
□□

زندگی شاید
یک خیابان درازست که هر روز زنی با زنبیلی از آن می‌گذرد
زندگی شاید
ریسمانیست که مردی با آن خود را از شاخه می‌آویزد
زندگی شاید طفلیست که از مدرسه بر می‌گردد

زندگی شاید افروختن سیگاری باشد، در فاصلهٔ رخوتناک دو
هم‌آغوشی
یا عبور گیج رهگذری باشد
که کلاه از سر بر می‌دارد
و به یک رهگذر دیگر بالبخندی بی معنی می‌گوید « صبح بخیر »

زندگی شاید آن لحظهٔ مسدودیست
که نگاه من، در نی نی چشمان تو خود را ویران می‌سازد
و دراین حسی است
که من آنرا با ادراک ماه و بادریافت ظلمت خواهم آمیخت

۲

در اتاقی که باندازهٔ یک تنهائیست
دل من
که بهاندازهٔ یک عشقت
به بهانههای سادهٔ خوشبختی خود مینگرد
به زوال زیبای گلها در گلدان
به نهالی که تو در باغچهٔ خانمان کاشتهای
و به آواز قناریها
که بهاندازهٔ یک پنجره میخوانند

آه ...
سهم من اینست
سهم من اینست
سهم من،
آسمانیست که آویختن پردهای آنرا از من میگیرد
سهم من پائین رفتن از یک پلهٔ مترو کست
و به چیزی در پوسیدگی و غربت واصل گشتن

سهم من گردش حزن آلودی در باغ خاطرههاست
ودر اندوه صدائی جان دادن که به من میگوید:
«دستهایت را
«دوست میدارم»

دستهایم را در باغچه میکارم
سبز خواهم شد، میدانم، میدانم، میدانم
وپرستوها در گودی انگشتان جوهریم
تخم خواهند گذاشت

۳

گوشواری بهدو گوشم می‌آویزم
از دو گیلاس سرخ همزاد
و به ناخن‌هایم برگ گل کوکب می‌چسبانم
کوچه‌ای هست که در آنجا
پسرانی که به من عاشق بودند ، هنوز
با همان موهای درهم و گردن‌های باریک و پاهای لاغر
به تبسم‌های معصوم دختر کی می‌اندیشند که یک‌شب او را
باد با خود برد

کوچه‌ای هست که قلب من آن را
از محله‌های کودکیم دزدیده‌ست

سفر حجمی در خط زمان
و به حجمی خط خشک زمان را آبستن کردن
حجمی از تصویری آگاه
که ز مهمانی یک آینه بر می‌گردد

و بدینسانست
که کسی می‌میرد
و کسی می‌ماند

□□

هیچ صیادی در جوی حقیری که به گودالی می‌ریزد ، مرواریدی
صید نخواهد کرد.

من
پری کوچک غمگینی را
می‌شناسم که در اقیانوسی مسکن دارد

۴

ودلش را دریك نی لبك چوبین

مینوازد آرام، آرام

پری كوچك غمگینی

كه شب از یك بوسه میمیرد

وسحرگاه از یك بوسه بدنیا خواهد آمد

» مردم چمنه طل من گوش میكنی «

» فردا مرا چو غم فراموش میكنی «

ه . ا . سایه

چون سنگها صدای مرا گوش میكنی

سنگی و ناشنیده فراموش میكنی

رگبار نوبهاری و خواب دریچه را

از ضربهای وسوسه مغشوش میكنی

دست مرا كه ساقهٔ سبز نوازش است

بابرگ های مرده همآغوش میكنی

گمراه تر ز روح شرابی و دیده را

در شعله مینشانی و مدهوش میكنی

ای ماهی طلائی مرداب خون من

خوش باد مستیت، كه مرا نوش میكنی

تودرهٔ بنقش غروبی كه روز را

برسینه میفشاری وخاموش میكنی

در سایمها، فروغ تو بنشست ورنگ باخت

اورا به سایه ازچه سیه پوش میكنی ؟

۵

ای مرز پر گهر ...

فاتح شدم

خود را به ثبت رساندم

خود را به نامی، در یک شناسنامه، مزین کردم

و هستیم به یک شماره مشخص شد

پس زنده باد ۶۷۸ صادره از بخش ۵ ساکن تهران

دیگر خیالم از همه سو راحت است

آغوش مهربان مام وطن

پستانک سوابق پر افتخار تاریخی

لالائی تمدن و فرهنگ

وجق وجق جقجقهٔ قانون ...

آه.

دیگر خیالم از همه سو راحت است

از فرط شادمانی

رفتم کنار پنجره، با اشتیاق، ششصد و هفتاد و هشت

بار هوا را که از غبار پهن

و بوی خاکروبه و ادرار، منقبض شده بود

درون سینه فرو دادم

و زیر ششصد و هفتاد و هشت قبض بدهکاری

و روی ششصد و هفتاد و هشت تقاضای کار نوشتم

فروغ فرخزاد

۶

در سرزمین شعر و گل و بلبل
موهبتیست زیستن، آنهم
وقتی که واقعیت موجود بودن تو پس از سال‌های
سال پذیرفته میشود

جائی که من
با اولین نگاه رسمی از لای پرده، ششصد و هفتاد و
هشت شاعر را می‌بینم
که، حقه‌بازها، همه در هیئت غریب گدایان
در لای خاکروبه، به دنبال وزن و قافیه میگردند
و ازصدای اولین قدم رسمی
یکباره، از میان لجن‌زارهای تیره، ششصد و هفتاد و
هشت بلبل مرموز

که از سر تفنن
خود را بشکل ششصد و هفتاد و هشت کلاغ سیاه
پیر در آورده‌اند
با تنبلی بسوی حاشیهٔ روز میپرند

و اولین نفس‌زدن رسمی
آغشته میشود به بوی ششصد و هفتاد و هشت شاخه
گل سرخ
محصول کارخانجات عظیم پلاسکو

موهبتیست زیستن، آری
در زادگاه شیخ ابودلقك كمانچه کش فوری
و شیخ ای دل ای دل تنبك تبار تنبوری
شهر ستارگان گران وزن ساقو باسن و پستان و
پشت جلد وهنر
گهواره مؤلفان فلسفهٔ «ه ای بابا بمنچه ولش كز

۷

مهد مسابقات المپیك موش ـ وای!
جائی که دست به هر دستگاه نقلی تصویر و صوت
میزنی، از آن
بوق نبوغ نابغه‌های تازه سال می‌آید
و برگزیدگان فکری ملت

وقتی که در کلاس اکابر حضور میابند
هریک به روی سینه، ششصدو هفتادو هشت کباب پز
برقی
و بر دو دست، ششصدو هفتادو هشت ساعت ناوزر ردیف
کرده و میدانند
که ناتوانی از خواص تهی کیسه بودنست، نه نادانی

فاتح شدم   بله فاتح شدم
اکنون به شادمانی این فتح
در پای آینه، با افتخار، ششصدو هفتادو هشت شمع
نسیه میافروزم
و میرم به روی طاقچه تا، با اجازه، چند کلامی
درباره فوائد قانون نی‌حیات بمعرض حضورتان برسانم
و اولین کلنگ ساختمان رفیع زندگیم را
همراه با طنین کف‌زدنی پرشور
بر فرق فرق خویش بکوبم
من زندهام، بله، مانند زنده رود، که یکروز زنده بود
و از تمام آنچه که در انحصار مردم زندمست، بهره
خواهم برد

من میتوانم از فردا
در کوچه‌های شهر، که سرشار از مواهب ملیست
و در میان سایه‌های سبکبار تیرهای تلگراف
گردش کنان قدم بردارم

و با غرور، ششصدو هفتادوهشت بار، بهدیوار مستراح
های عمومی بنویسم
خط نوشتم که خر کند خنده

من میتوانم از فردا
همچون وطنپرست غیوری
سهمی از ایدهآل عظیمی که اجتماع
هر چارشنبه بعدازظهر، آنرا
با اشتیاق و دلهره دنبال میکند
در قلب و مغز خویش داشته باشم
سهمی از آن هزار هزار هوسپرور هزار ریالی
که میتوان بهمصرف یخچال و مبلو پرده رساندش
یا آنکه در ازای ششصدو هفتادو هشت رأی طبیعی
آنرا شبی به ششصدو هفتادو هشت مرد وطن بخشید

من میتوانم از فردا
در پستوی مغازهٔ خاچیک
بعداز فرو کشیدن چندین نفس، ز چند گرم جنس
دست اول خالص
و صرف چند بادیه پیسی کولای ناخالص
و پخش چند یاحق و یاهو و وغ وغ و هوهو
رسماً بهمجمع فضلای فکور و فضلهای فاضل
روشنفکر
و پیروان مکتب داخ داخ تاراخ تاراخ بپیوندم
و طرح اولین رمان بزرگم را
که درحوالی سنهٔ یکهزارو ششصدو هفتادو هشت
شمسی تبریزی
رسماً به زیر دستگاه تهیدست چاپ خواهد رفت

۹

بر هر دو پشت ششصدو هفتادو هشت پاکت
اشنوی اصل ویژه بریزم

من میتوانم از فردا
با اعتماد کامل
خودرا برای ششصدو هفتادو هشت دوره بهیک
دستگاه مسند مخمل پوش
در مجلس تجمع و تأمین آتیه
یا مجلس سپاس و ثنا میهمان کنم
زیرا کاممن تمام مندرجات مجلهٔ هنر و دانش ـ و
تملق و کرنش را میخوانم
و شیوهٔ « درست نوشتن » را میدانم

من در میان تودهٔ سازندهای قدم بعرصهٔ هستی
نهادهام
که گرچه نان ندارد، اما بجای آن
میدان دید باز و وسیعی دارد
که مرزهای فعلی جغرافیائیش
از جانب شمال ، به میدان پرطراوت و سبز تیر
و از جنوب، به میدان باستانی اعدام
و درمناطق پر ازدحام، به میدان توپخانه رسیدهست

و در پناه آسمان درخشان و امن امنیتش
از صبح تا غروب، ششصدو هفتادو هشت قوی قوی
هیکل گچی
بهاتفاق ششصدو هفتادو هشت فرشته

ـ آنهم فرشتهٔ از خاك و گل سرشته ـ
به تبلیغ طرحهای سکون وسکوت مشغولند

□□

فاتح شدم   بله فاتح شدم
پس زنده باد ۶۷۸ صادره از بخش ۵ ساکن تهران
که درپناه پشتکار و اراده
به آنچنان مقام رفیعی رسیده است، که در چارچوب
پنجره ای
در ارتفاع ششصدو هفتادو هشت متری سطح زمین
قرار گرفتست

و افتخار این را دارد
که میتواند از همان دریچه ـ نه از راه پلکان ـ
خود را
دیوانهوار بهدامان مهربان مام وطن سرنگون کند

و آخرین وصیتش اینست
که در ازای ششصدو هفتادو هشت سکه، حضرت
استاد آبراهام صبا
مرثیهای بهقافیهٔ کشك در رثای حیاتش رقم زند

۱۱

ایمان بیاوریم به‌آغاز فصل سرد...

و این منم
زنی تنها
در آستانه‌ی فصلی سرد
در ابتدای درک هستی آلوده‌ی زمین
و یأس ساده و غمناک آسمان
و ناتوانی این دستهای سیمانی.

زمان گذشت
زمان گذشت و ساعت چهار بار نواخت
چهار بار نواخت
امروز روز اول دیماه است
من راز فصل‌ها را میدانم
و حرف لحظه‌ها را میفهم
نجات‌دهنده در گور خفته است
و خاک، خاک پذیرنده
اشارتیست به‌آرامش

زمان گذشت و ساعت چهار بار نواخت.

در کوچه باد میاید
در کوچه باد میاید
و من به‌جفت‌گیری گل‌ها میاندیشم
به غنچه‌هایی با ساق‌های لاغر کم‌خون

۱۲

و این زمان خستهی مسلول

و مردی از کنار درختان خیس میگذرد

مردی که رشتههای آبی رگهایش

مانند مارهای مرده از دوسوی گلوگاهش

بالا خزیدهاند

و در شقیقههای منقلبش آن هجای خونین را

تکرار میکنند

ـ سلام

ـ سلام

و من به جفتگیری گلها میاندیشم.

در آستانهی فصلی سرد

در محفل عزای آینهها

و اجتماع سوگوار تجربههای پریدهرنگ

و این غروب بارور شده از دانش سکوت

چگونه میشود به آنکسی که میرود اینسان

صبور،

سنگین،

سرگردان.

فرمان ایست داد.

چگونه میشود به مرد گفت که او زنده نیست، او هیچوقت

زنده نبودهست.

در کوچه باد می‌آید
کلاغ‌های منفرد انزوا
در باغ‌های پیر کسالت می‌چرخند
و نردبام
چه ارتفاع حقیری دارد.

آن‌ها تمام ساده‌لوحی یک قلب را
با خود به‌قصر قصه‌ها بردند
و اکنون دیگر
دیگر چگونه یک‌نفر به‌رقص برخواهد خاست
و گیسوان کودکیش را
در آب‌های جاری خواهد ریخت
و سیب را که سرانجام چیده است و بوئیده است
در زیر پا لگد خواهد کرد؟

ای یار، ای یگانه‌ترین یار
چه ابرهای سیاهی در انتظار روز میهمانی خورشیدند.

انگار در مسیری از تجسم پرواز بود که یکروز آن پرنده
نمایان شد
انگار از خطوط سبز تخیل بودند
آن برگ‌های تازه که در شهوت نسیم نفس می‌زدند
انگار
آن شعله‌ی بنفش که در ذهن پاک پنجره‌ها می‌سوخت
چیزی بجز تصور معصومی از چراغ نبود.

۱۴

در کوچه باد می‌آید

این ابتدای ویرانیست

آن روزهم که دست‌های تو ویران شدند باد می‌آمد

ستاره‌های عزیز

ستاره‌های مقوائی عزیز

وقتی در آسمان، دروغ وزیدن میگیرد

دیگر چگونه میشود به‌سوره‌های رسولان سرشکسته پناه
آورد؟

ما مثل مرده‌های هزاران هزارساله به‌هم میرسیم و آنگاه
خورشید بر تمامی اجساد ما قضاوت خواهد کرد.

من سردم است

من سردم است و انگار هیچوقت گرم نخواهم شد

ای یار ای یگانه‌ترین یار «آن شراب مگر چند ساله بود؟»

نگاه‌کن که در اینجا

زمان چه وزنی دارد

و ماهیان چگونه گوشت‌های مرا میبوند

چرا مرا همیشه در ته دریا نگاهمیداری؟

من سردم است و از گوشواره‌های صدف بیزارم

من سردم است و میدانم

که از تمامی اوهام سرخ یک شقایق وحشی

جز چند قطره خون

چیزی بجا نخواهد ماند.

۱۵

خطوط را رها خواهم کرد

و همچنین شمارش اعداد را رها خواهم کرد

و از میان شکل‌های هندسی محدود

به پهنه‌های حسی وسعت پناه خواهم برد

من عریانم، عریانم، عریانم

مثل سکوت‌های میان کلام‌های محبت عریانم

و زخم‌های من همه از عشق است

از عشق، عشق، عشق.

من این جزیره‌ی سرگردان را

از انقلاب اقیانوس

و انفجار کوه گذر داده‌ام

و تکه‌تکه شدن، راز آن وجود متحدی بود

که از حقیرترین ذره‌هایش آفتاب به‌دنیا آمد.

سلام ای شب معصوم!

سلام ای شبی که چشم‌های گرگ‌های بیابان را

به حفره‌های استخوانی ایمان و اعتماد بدل می‌کنی

و در کنار جویبارهای تو، ارواح بیدها

ارواح مهربان تبرها را می‌بویند

من از جهان بی‌تفاوتی فکرها و حرف‌ها و صداها میایم

و این جهان به‌لانه‌ی ماران ماننده است

و این جهان پر از صدای حرکت پاهای مردمیست

که همچنان که ترا میبوسند
در ذهن خود طناب دار ترا میبافند.

سلام ای شب معصوم!

میان پنجره و دیدن
همیشه فاصله ایست.
چرا نگاه نکردم؟
مانند آن زمان کـه مردی از کنار درختان خیس گــذر
میکرد...

چرا نگاه نکردم؟
انگار مادرم گریسته بود آنشب
آنشب که من به درد رسیدم و نطفه شکل گرفت
آنشب که من عروس خوشه های اقاقی شدم
آنشب که اصفهان پر از طنین کاشی آبی بود،
و آنکسی که نیمه ی من بود، به درون نطفه ی من بازگشته بود
و من در آینه میدیدمش،
که مثل آینه پاکیزه بود و روشن بود
و ناگهان صدایم کرد
و من عروس خوشه های اقاقی شدم...

۱۷

انگار مادرم گریسته بود آنشب.
چه روشنائی بیهوده‌ای در این دریچه‌ی مسدود سرکشید
چرا نگاه نکردم؟
تمام لحظه‌های سعادت میدانستند
که دست‌های تو ویران خواهد شد
و من نگاه نکردم
تا آن زمان که پنجره‌ی ساعت
گشوده شد و آن قناری غمگین چهار بار نواخت
چهار بار نواخت
و من به آن زن کوچک برخوردم
که چشمهایش، مانند لانه‌های خالی سیمرغان بودند
و آنچنان که در تحرک ران‌هایش میرفت
گوئی بکارت رؤیای پرشکوه مرا
با خود بسوی بستر شب میبرد.

آیا دوباره گیسوانم را
در باد شانه خواهم زد؟
آیا دوباره باغچه‌ها را بنفشه خواهم کاشت؟
و شمعدانی‌ها را
در آسمان پشت پنجره خواهم گذاشت؟
آیا دوباره روی لیوان‌ها خواهم رقصید؟
آیا دوباره زنگ در مرا بسوی انتظار صدا خواهد برد؟

۱۸

به مادرم گفتم: «دیگر تمام شد.»
گفتم: «همیشه پیش از آنکه فکر کنی اتفاق میافتد
باید برای روزنامه تسلیتی بفرستیم»

انسان پوک
انسان پوک پر از اعتماد
نگاه کن که دندانهایش
چگونه وقت جویدن سرود میخوانند
و چشمهایش
چگونه وقت خیره شدن میدرند
و او چگونه از کنار درختان خیس میگذرد:
صبور،
سنگین،
سرگردان.

در ساعت چهار
در لحظهای که رشتههای آبی رگهایش
مانند مارهای مرده از دو سوی گلوگاهش
بالا خزیدهاند
و در شقیقههای منقلبش آن هجای خونین را
تکرار میکنند
ـ سلام
ـ سلام
آیا تو
هرگز آن چهار لالهی آبی را
بوئیدهای؟...

۱۹

زمان گذشت

زمان گذشت و شب روی شاخه‌های لخت اقاقی افتاد
شب پشت شیشه‌های پنجره سرمیخورد
و با زبان سردش
ته مانده‌های روز رفته را به‌درون میکشد

من از کجا میایم؟

من از کجا میایم؟
که اینچنین به بوی شب آغشته‌ام؟
هنوز خاک مزارش تازه‌ست
مزار آن دو دست سبز جوان را میگویم...

چه مهربان بودی ای یار، ای یگانه‌ترین یار
چه مهربان بودی وقتی دروغ میگفتی
چه مهربان بودی وقتی که پلک‌های آینه‌ها را می‌بستی
و چلچراغ‌ها را
از ساقه‌های سیمی میچیدی
و در سیاهی ظالم مرا بسوی چراگاه عشق میبردی
تاآن بخارِ گیجی‌که دنباله‌ی خریق عطش بود بر چمن خواب
مینشست

و آن ستاره‌های مقوایی
به‌گرد لایتناهی میچرخیدند.
چرا کلام را به‌صدا گفتند؟

چرا نگاه را به‌خانه‌ی دیدار میهمان کردند!
چرا نوازش را
به‌حجب گیسوان باکرگی بردند؟
نگاه کن که در اینجا
چگونه جان آنکسی که باکلام سخن گفت
و بانگاه نواخت
و بانوازش از رمیدن آرامید
به تیرهای توهم
مصلوب گشته است.
و جای پنج شاخه‌ی انگشتهای تو
که مثل پنج حرف حقیقت بودند
چگونه روی گونه او مانده‌ست.

سکوت چیست، چیست، چیست ای یگانه‌ترین یار؟
سکوت چیست بجز حرف‌های ناگفته
من از گفتن میمانم، اما زبان گنجشگان
زبان زندگی جمله‌های جاری جشن طبیعتست.
زبان گنجشگان یعنی: بهار. برگ. بهار.
زبان گنجشگان یعنی: نسیم. عطر. نسیم.
زبان گنجشگان در کارخانه میمیرد.

این کیست این کسی که روی جاده‌ی ابدیت
بسوی لحظه‌ی توحید میرود
و ساعت همیشگیش را
با منطق ریاضی تفریق‌ها و تفرقه‌ها کوک میکند.

این کیست این کسی که بانگ خروسان را
آغاز قلب روز نمیداند
آغاز بوی ناشتایی میداند
این کیست این کسی که تاج عشق به‌سر دارد
و در میان جامه‌های عروسی پوسیده‌ست.

پس آفتاب سرانجام
در یک زمان واحد
بر هر دو قطب ناامید نتابید.
تو از طنین کاشی آبی تهی شدی.

و من چنان پرم که روی صدایم نماز میخوانند...

جنازه‌های خوشبخت
جنازه‌های ملول
جنازه‌های ساکت متفکر
جنازه‌های خوش‌برخورد، خوش‌پوش، خوش‌خوراک
در ایستگاههای وقت‌های معین
و در زمینه‌ی مشکوک نورهای موقت
و شهوت خرید میوه‌های فاسد بیهودگی...
آه،
چه مردمانی در چارراهها نگران حوادثند
و این صدای سوت‌های توقف
در لحظه‌ای که باید، باید، باید
مردی به‌زیر چرخ‌های زمان له شود
مردی که از کنار درختان خیس میگذرد...

۲۲

من از کجا میایم؟

به‌مادرم گفتم: «دیگر تمام شد»
گفتم: «همیشه پیش از آنکه فکر کنی اتفاق میافتد
باید برای روزنامه تسلیتی بفرستیم.»

سلام ای غرابت تنهائی
اتاق را به‌تو تسلیم میکنم
چرا که ابرهای تیره همیشه
پیغمبران آیه‌های تازه تطهیر‌ند
و در شهادت یک شمع
راز منوری است که آنرا
آن آخرین و آن کشیده‌ترین شعله خوب میداند.

ایمان بیاوریم
ایمانَ بیاوریم به‌آغاز فصل سرد
ایمان بیاوریم به‌ویرانه‌های باغ‌های تخیل
به‌داس‌های واژگون شده‌ی بیکار
و دانه‌های زندانی.
نگاه کن که چه برفی میبارد...

شاید حقیقت آن دو دست جوان بود، آن دو دست جوان
که زیر بارش یکریز برف مدفون شد
و سال دیگر، وقتی بهار
باآسمان پشت پنجره همخوابه میشود
و در تنش فوران میکنند

فواره‌های سبز ساقه‌های سبکبار
شکوفه خواهد داد ای یار، ای یگانه‌ترین یار

ایمان بیاوریم به آغاز فصل سرد....

آیه‌های زمینی

آنگاه
خورشید سرد شد
و برکت از زمین‌ها رفت

و سبزه‌ها به صحراها خشکیدند
و ماهیان به دریاها خشکیدند
و خاک مردگانش را
زان پس به خود نپذیرفت

شب در تمام پنجره‌های پریده رنگ
مانند یک تصور مشکوک
پیوسته در تراکم و طغیان بود
و راه‌ها ادامهٔ خود را
در تیرگی رها کردند

دیگر کسی به عشق نیندیشید
دیگر کسی به فتح نیندیشید
و هیچکس
دیگر به هیچ چیز نیندیشید

در غارهای تنهائی
بیهودگی به دنیا آمد
خون بوی بنگ و افیون میداد
زنهای باردار
نوزادهای بی سر زائیدند
و گاهوارها از شرم
به گورها پناه آوردند

چه روزگار تلخ و سیاهی
نان، نیروی شگفت رسالت را
مغلوب کرده بود
پیغمبران گرسنه و مغلوک
از وعده گاههای الهی گریختند
و بره‌های گمشده
دیگر صدای هی هی چوپانی را
در بهت دشتها نشنیدند

در دیدگان آینه‌ها گوئی
حرکت و رنگها و تصاویر
وارونه منعکس میگشت
و بر فراز سر دلقکان پست
و چهرهٔ وقیح فواحش
یک هالهٔ مقدس نورانی
مانند چتر مشتعلی میسوخت

۲۵

مرداب‌های الکل
با آن بخارهای گس مسموم
انبوه بی‌تحرك روشنفكران را
به ژرفنای خویش کشیدند
و موشهای موذی
اوراق زرنگار کتب را
در گنجه‌های کهنه جویدند

خورشید مرده بود
خورشید مرده بود، و فردا
در ذهن کودکان
مفهوم گنگ گمشده‌ای داشت
آنها غرابت این لفظ کهنه را
در مشق‌های خود
بالكۀ درشت سیاهی
تصویر مینمودند

مردم،
گروه ساقط مردم
دلمرده و تکیده و مبهوت
در زیر بار شوم جسدهاشان
از غربتی بغربت دیگر میرفتند
ومیل دردناك جنایت
در دستهایشان متورم میشد

گاهی جرقه‌ای، جرقۀ ناچیزی
این اجتماع ساکت بیجان را

یکباره از درون متلاشی میکرد
آنها بهم هجوم میآوردند
مردان گلوی یکدیگر را
با کارد میدریدند
و در میان بستری از خون
با دختران نابالغ
همخوابه میشدند

آنها غریق وحشت خود بودند
و حس ترسناک گنهکاری
ارواح کور و کودنشان را
مفلوج کرده بود

پیوسته در مراسم اعدام
وقتی طناب دار
چشمان پرتشنج محکومی را
از کاسه با فشار به بیرون میریخت
آنها بهخود فرو میرفتند
و از تصور شهوتناکی
اعصاب پیر و خستهشان تیر میکشید

اما همیشه در حواشی میدانها
این جانیان کوچک را میدیدی
که ایستاده اند
وخیره گشتهاند
بهریزش مداوم فوارههای آب

□□

شاید هنوز هم
در پشت چشمهای لهشده، در عمق انجماد

۲۷

یک چیز نیم زندهٔ مغشوش
برجای مانده بود
که در تلاش بی ‌رمقش می‌خواست
ایمان بیاورد به‌پاکی آواز آبها
شاید، ولی چه خالی بی‌پایانی
خورشید مرده بود
و هیچکس نمی‌دانست
که نام آن کبوتر غمگین
کز قلبها گریخته، ایمانست

□□

آه، ای صدای زندانی
آیا شکوه یأس تو هرگز
از هیچ سوی این شب منفور
نقبی بسوی نور نخواهد زد ؟
آه، ای صدای زندانی
ای آخرین صدای صداها...

عاشقانه

ای شب از رؤیای تو رنگین شده
سینه از عطر توام سنگین شده
ای به روی چشم من گسترده خویش
شادیم بخشیده از اندوه بیش
همچو بارانی که شوید جسم خاک
هستیم ز آلودگی‌ها کرده پاک

۲۸

ای تپش‌های تن سوزان من
آتشی در سایهٔ مژگان من
ای ز گندمزارها سرشارتر
ای ز زرّین شاخه‌ها پر بارتر
ای در بگشوده بر خورشیدها
در هجوم ظلمت تردیدها
با توأم دیگر ز دردی بیم نیست
هست اگر ، جز درد خوشبختیم نیست

این دل تنگ من و این‌بار نور؟
های‌وهوی زندگی در قعر گور ؟

ای دوچشمانت چمنزاران من
داغ چشمت خورده بر چشمان من
پیش از اینت گر که در خود داشتم
هر کسی را کو تو می‌انگاشتم

درد تاریکیست درد خواستن
رفتن و بیهوده خود را کاستن
سر نهادن بر سیه دل سینه‌ها
سینه آلودن به چرک کینه‌ها
در نوازش ، نیش ماران یافتن
زهر در لبخند یـاران یـافتن
زر نهادن در کف طرّارهـا
گمشدن در پهنهٔ بـازارهـا

آه، ای با جان من آمیخته
ای مرا از گور من انگیخته

چون ستاره ، با دو بال زرنشان
آمده از دور دست آسمان
از تو تنهائیم خاموشی گرفت
پیکرم بوی هم‌آغوشی گرفت
جوی خشک سینه‌ام را آب تو
بستر رگ‌هام را سیلاب تو
در جهانی اینچنین سرد و سیاه
با قدمهایت قدمهایم براه

ای به زیر پوستم پنهان شده
همچو خون در پوستم جوشان شده
گیسویم را از نوازش سوخته
گونه‌هام از هرم خواهش سوخته
آه، ای بیگانه با پیراهنم
آشنای سبزه‌زاران تنم
آه، ای روشن طلوع بی‌غروب
آفتاب سرزمین‌های جنوب
آه ، آه ای از سحر شاداب‌تر
از بهاران تازه‌تر سیراب‌تر
عشق دیگر نیست این، این‌خیره‌گیست
چلچراغی در سکوت و تیره‌گیست
عشق چون در سینه‌ام بیدار شد
از طلب پا تا سرم ایثار شد

این دگر من نیستم، من نیستم
حیف از آن عمری که با من زیستم
ای لبانم بوسه‌گاه بوسه‌ات
خیره چشمانم به راه بوسه‌ات
ای تشنج‌های لذت در تنم

ای خطوط پیکرت پیراهنم
آه میخواهم که بشکافم ز هم
شادیم یکدم بیالاید به غم
آه، میخواهم که برخیزم ز جای
همچو ابری اشک ریزم های های

این دل تنگ من و این دود عود؟
در شبستان، زخمه‌های چنگ و رود؟
این فضای خالی و پروازها؟
این شب خاموش و این آوازها؟

□□

ای نگاهت لای لائی سحر بار
گاهوار کودکان بیقرار
ای نفسهایت نسیم نیمخواب
شسته از من لرزه‌های اضطراب
خفته در لبخند فرداهای من
رفته تا اعماق دنیاهای من

ای مرا با شور شعر آمیخته
اینهمه آتش به شعرم ریخته
چون تب عشقم چنین افروختی
لاجرم شعرم به آتش سوختی

۳۱

ADDENDUM
Selected Poems in Persian